Exploring the *Catechism of the Catholic Church*

William H. Shannon

CINCINNATI, OHIO

Nihil Obstat: Rev. Thomas Richstatter, O.F.M.
Rev. Edward J. Gratsch

Imprimi Potest: Rev. John Bok, O.F.M., Provincial

Imprimatur: Most Reverend Carl K. Moeddel, V.G.
Archdiocese of Cincinnati, November 29, 1994

The *nihil obstat* and *imprimatur* are a declaration that a book is considered to be free from doctrinal or moral error. It is not implied that those who have granted the *nihil obstat* and *imprimatur* agree with the contents, opinions or statements expressed.

Book design by Mary Alfieri

Cover design by Leslie Brod

ISBN 0-86716-234-1

Published by St. Anthony Messenger Press
Printed in the U.S.A.

Contents

INTRODUCTION

What Is the *Catechism of the Catholic Church?*

> *I declare [the* Catechism of the Catholic Church*] to be a sure norm for teaching the faith and thus a valid and legitimate instrument for ecclesial communion. May it serve the renewal to which the Holy Spirit ceaselessly calls the Church of God, the Body of Christ, on her pilgrimage to the undiminished light of the Kingdom!*
> —Pope John Paul II (Catechism, #3)

The word *catechism* opens up many windows of memory for Catholics who lived in the pre-Vatican II Church. My fondest memory is the picture of my non-Catholic father "hearing my catechism" almost every night and my dutiful recitation of words that probably neither of us understood. Memorizing the answers to the questions about Catholic belief did at least get me through Sister Teresina's catechism class the next day; and if the whole class did well through the week, we were rewarded with a Bible story on Friday.

That method was great for discipline and a wonderful way of developing the memory; but precious little intelligible catechesis—faith education—took place. And it is hard to buy the argument that, even though you did not understand it then, it would become clear later. No, as a priest and educator today I know that religious instruction has to reach a person where he or she is *now* or it is not authentic catechesis.

Fortunately, the new *Catechism of the Catholic Church* is not intended to develop our memories. (Such an approach would pose a formidable task indeed, since the catechism runs to 803 pages!) Rather, it is a gift from the teaching authorities of the Church (the *magisterium*) to the faithful in order that they may more fully understand the riches of the salvation God has offered to us in Jesus Christ.

How the Catechism *Came to Be*

On January 25, 1985, Pope John Paul II called an extraordinary assembly of the Synod of Bishops to commemorate the twentieth anniversary of the conclusion of the Second Vatican Council. At this meeting it was proposed that a catechism or compendium of Catholic doctrine on faith and morals be composed to serve as a source book for local catechisms to be written in countries around the world.

In 1986 the Pope appointed a commission of twelve bishops to carry out the task of drawing up such a source book under the leadership of Cardinal Joseph Ratzinger, head of the Congregation for the Doctrine of the Faith. The commission was made up of experienced and distinguished Church leaders representing Europe (both East and West), the United States, South America, Africa and the Eastern Catholic Churches of the Middle East. Two Americans were on the commission: Cardinal William Baum of Washington, D.C., and Cardinal Bernard Law of Boston.

The task of the commission was to work out the general structure and character of the *Catechism*. They also followed the text as it gradually took shape through nine successive drafts. These drafts were created by an editorial board of seven bishops from Spain, France, Italy, England, the United States (Archbishop Levada of Portland, Oregon), Lebanon and Austria. Bishop Schonborn of Austria acted as intermediary between the commission and the editorial committee.

A first draft was completed in the spring of 1988. This text was written in Latin and translated into various languages. In November 1989 this first draft, called the *Catechism for the Universal Church*, was sent to all the bishops for their suggestions and criticisms.

What resulted was a first-rate exercise of collegiality. The recommendations sent in by the bishops around the world were given serious consideration and significant changes were made in succeeding drafts. The Commission for the Catechism and its editorial committee completed their work on February 14, 1992. The ninth and last draft bore a different name: *Catechism of the Catholic Church.* This normative text, from which all translations are made, was written in French. Pope John Paul II approved it on June 25, 1992.

In the Vatican Palace, on December 10, 1992, while the Sistine Choir sang Palestrina's Mass in honor of the Blessed Virgin Mary, Pope John Paul II gave the new *Catechism* to the world.

The Intended Audience

The original intent of the *Catechism* was to help diocesan bishops, bishops' conferences and catechism writers draw up new local catechisms. These would take cultural differences into consideration and, at the same time, preserve the unity of the Church's faith. The Prologue to the *Catechism*, while preserving the original intent, also suggests that the *Catechism* will be a help to catechists and useful reading for all the faithful.

The fact that the English translation hit the best-seller list soon after publication indicates that it will reach a wide audience. One cannot help but wonder if this extension of the audience far beyond the original intent will leave little incentive to create local catechisms. Yet the authors of the *Catechism* make clear that such local catechisms are indispensable because of the need to adapt doctrinal content and catechetical methods to the differences in culture, age, spiritual growth, and social and ecclesial conditions that exist among the people of God.

Goals of the *Catechism*

The *Catechism* is a source book that surely and authentically articulates the teachings of the Catholic Church. Its primary intent is to *inform.* A person who reads it should have at the end of the reading a reasonably clear understanding of what is officially taught by the Church.

Yet, sensitive readers will face an immediate problem.

Having read such a huge amount of material, they will instinctively realize that all of it cannot be of equal importance. How, they will want to know, can we discover some way of distinguishing what is of primary importance from what is of secondary importance?

Unfortunately, the *Catechism* is not completely clear on this issue. But it does do two helpful things: (1) It puts in smaller type matters clearly considered of lesser importance. (There is still an enormous amount of larger type.) (2) The *Catechism* quotes a statement from Vatican II to make it easier for you and me to strike a balance between what we need to be ready to die for and what is of lesser importance: "There exists an order or 'hierarchy' of truths, since they vary in their connection with the foundation of the Christian faith" (*Decree on Ecumenism*, #11).

This text is helpful; still, it creates a problem of its own: Neither the Council nor the Catechism defines the "foundation of Christian faith." It seems important to make an attempt to identify it.

Several answers are possible. I would say that the foundation of Christian faith is the resurrection of Jesus. I think this is what Pope Paul VI meant when he said in his 1975 encyclical, *Evangelization in the Modern World*: "Evangelization will always contain—as the foundation, center and at the same time summit of its dynamism—a clear proclamation that, in Jesus Christ, the Son of God, made man, who died and rose from the dead, salvation is offered to all men as a gift of God's grace and mercy" (#27). Much closer in time to the foundation reality itself are the words of Pope Paul's namesake, who said that "if Christ has not been raised, your faith is futile and you are still in your sins" (1 Corinthians 15:17).

This position fits with what the *Catechism* says: "The Resurrection of Jesus is the crowning truth of our faith in Christ, a faith believed and lived as the central truth by the first Christian community; handed on as *fundamental* by Tradition; established by the documents of the New Testament; and preached, as an essential part of the Paschal Mystery, along with the cross" (#638, emphasis added).

From this foundation, I suggest, flow Baptism, which incorporates us into Jesus' death and resurrection, and the Eucharist, which celebrates those events. Baptism and Eucharist give birth to the Church. Members of this Church are linked to one another in a communion called to promote justice, goodness and peace.

One could go on and on, showing how the beliefs we ascribe to, the moral commitments we strive to follow and the spirituality we try to live can be traced back to the Resurrection as the foundation of Christian faith. I offer this as a possible unifying truth with which to approach the material in the Catechism. Other truths might also be chosen as foundational: for example, our belief in a Trinitarian God, or our belief in the unconditional love of Jesus and his command that we imitate that love.

If the Catechism's primary goal is to offer a good bit of information about Catholic beliefs, its second goal, rivaling the first in importance, is to offer a strong challenge to those whose privileged responsibility it is to teach Catholic faith. It calls them to foster and deepen the faith-life of the Church community by focusing on doctrinal, moral and spiritual content as the base on which to build true Christian community.

What Is a Catechism?

The *Catechism of the Catholic Church* belongs to a unique literary form. What is a catechism? What role have catechisms played in the process of handing on the faith?

A catechism is a book of unchallenged answers. Even when a catechism follows the question-answer format so familiar to many from the *Baltimore Catechism* (the *Catechism of the Catholic Church* does not), the *answers*, not the experience of people, dictate what the questions will be. A catechism poses a built-in danger of giving the reader a kind of smug sense of being "right." One might mistakenly think there is no need for the student or teacher to struggle with the questions, as they would in other areas of study, because the answers are all there. There are no debates to be engaged in, for there are never two sides to an issue.

Certain and *beyond challenge* written clear over every page: This is what gives a catechism its unique flavor and identity. A book characterized by such unyielding confidence in itself can be a help for Catholics. In a world faced with all sorts of uncertainties, it can be a comfort to repose in the security of a catechism. On the other hand, this inflexible air of confidence can also pose a problem. Life continually poses new questions—questions that never occurred to the writers. How are Catholics to deal with such questions? Will a closed-minded mentality, which the catechism may tend to encourage in some people, leave them unprepared to face the unexpected question?

This is not to say that one cannot take the light of faith gained from a catechism and use it to shed light on new situations and problems. The questions still remain, however: Does our experience of these new situations and problems in any way illuminate the truths of faith? Do they help us to see aspects of those truths we never saw before? Do new questions and situations stretch our minds and deepen our understanding of what God is trying to teach us?

A Very Brief History of Catechisms

The first catechisms (somewhat like the Gospels) were spoken before they were written. They began as instructions given to the newly baptized by such Fathers of the Church as Cyril of Jerusalem or John Chrysostom of Constantinople, and later were committed to writing. Later catechisms (such as the *Roman Catechism*, conceived by the Council of Trent, and the United States bishops' *Baltimore Catechism*) reversed this process. They were written first and then became the source from which catechists drew to give instructions to children, young people and interested adults.

In other words, in the beginning catechesis came first, rising out of the experience of the catechist and the community; only later was it put into a written document or "catechism." Later catechisms, on the other hand, were written first out of the experience of the Church, then used by catechists. What should be clear is that, whether catechesis or catechism comes first, the key to effective catechizing is the catechist.

Catechist, *catechesis* and *catechize* all come from a single Greek verb. If you check this verb in a good Greek dictionary, you will make an intriguing discovery: This verb's first meaning is "to charm, to fascinate." Its second meaning is "to teach orally, to instruct." If you put these two meanings together in a Christian context, the catechist is one who "teaches orally" in such a way as to dazzle, charm, fascinate those who are being catechized. Catechesis, in other words, cannot be reduced to the contents of a book (a catechism) which the catechist simply communicates to the students (the catechized). An experience of that kind would be dreary indeed! For, frankly, a catechism is not an exciting text. Words like *dull* and *boring* are more likely to come to mind in describing it. At best, it is not a lively book, not the kind you would take for leisure reading on a trip.

A catechism comes alive only through the persons of committed catechists who are on fire with the truths of faith that the book contains, who embody the truths and values they teach, who proclaim from their very bones a faith that is their own and that they want to share with others.

This is not to deny the value of catechisms. It is simply to say that they achieve their potential only when translated by teachers and parents into the readers' life-contexts. Catechisms are prose yearning to be poetry. It is the catechist who, through the use of narrative, images, symbols and experiences of faith, makes this transformation possible.

The work of catechists will be much more fruitful if the catechisms they use have been drawn up in the local Church and reflect the cultural and social makeup of a particular area. Local catechisms ought to be brief. It is up to catechists to flesh out their leanness.

Catechisms of this sort will also meet the need of at least two other groups in the Church: (1) adults, Catholic or not, who wish to explore questions of faith but who have little inkling of the truths of Catholic faith and no idea of the organic unity of the beliefs professed by Catholics; (2) new parents who come for instruction in preparation for the baptism of a child and who need a clear and coherent presentation of Catholic faith.

Contents of the Catechism of the Catholic Church

The *Catechism of the Catholic Church* follows the traditional outline of a catechism. Like the *Roman Catechism* of the Council of Trent, it is divided into four parts: Creed, Sacraments, Commandments and Prayer.

A charming feature of the *Catechism* is that color photographs of art works introduce each part and suggest its basic theme. Part One (the Creed) features a fragment of a fresco from the catacombs of Priscilla in Rome—the most ancient image of the Virgin Mary in existence. She is pictured holding her Son and with a star over her head. At her left is a prophet, probably Balaam, announcing "a star shall come out of Jacob" (Numbers 24:17). The image introduces the central theme of the Creed: the incarnate Son of God, born of the Virgin and given to all humankind.

Part Two (Liturgy and the Sacraments) is introduced by a fresco from the Church of Saints Marcellinus and Peter in Rome. It depicts Jesus' meeting with the woman who for many years had suffered from hemorrhage (see Mark 5:25-34). The woman is touching the hem of Jesus' cloak. Jesus' hand is extended toward her as he realizes that power has gone out from him. What the photograph says is that the sacraments are visible signs of the saving and healing power of Jesus that come forth now from the Risen One present among us.

The section on the Commandments (Part Three) offers the central section of a Roman sarcophagus dating from the year 539. Christ is portrayed in glory. The apostles Peter and Paul receive from him two scrolls, representing the twofold Great Commandment: love of God and love of neighbor.

Part Four (Prayer and the Our Father) opens with a colored miniature from Mount Athos in Greece. It depicts a desert scene. Jesus is absorbed in prayer to God, who appears in the upper right-hand corner. The disciples are there, too, but they stand in awe at a respectful distance. Only after Jesus has finished his prayer do they make their request: "Lord, teach us to pray" (see Luke 11:1).

The wealth of material in the *Catechism* is not adequately conveyed by its four-fold division. Each of these divisions has an important introductory section that puts its topic in context. Thus Part One begins with a section on revelation, the initiative whereby God addresses people, and on faith, humanity's response to that revelation (#26-184).

Part Two has a fine section on liturgy (#1066-1209), which introduces the discussion of the seven sacraments. Liturgy is seen as the revelation, communication and acknowledgment of the blessings God has visited on humankind. These blessings are proclaimed in Scripture from "the liturgical poem of the first creation" (Genesis) to the "songs of the heavenly Jerusalem" (Revelation). Liturgy celebrates the presence of Christ in his Church here and now—in the community of his people, in his minister, in his word proclaimed and especially in the Eucharistic bread and wine. Liturgy is the action of the Holy Spirit, "the Church's living memory" (#1099), who makes present among us the mystery of Christ.

Part Three, which deals with the Ten Commandments, is introduced with a long section on the Christian way (#1691-2051). It is made up of three chapters. Chapter One, "The Dignity of the Human Person," deals with such topics as the image of God, human happiness, freedom, the morality of human acts, moral conscience and sin. The second, "The Human Community," discusses the person and community, participation in social life, social justice, human solidarity. Chapter Three, "God's Salvation: Law and Grace," includes such topics as the moral law, the new law of the gospel, grace and justification, the Church as mother and teacher.

Part Four, "Christian Prayer" has no special introduction, although its first section, "Prayer in the Christian Life" (#2558-2758), prepares for a study of the Lord's Prayer (#2759-2865). Many aspects of prayer are discussed: prayer in the Scriptures and in the life of the Church, the sources of prayer, the ways people have prayed, different schools of prayer, the role of the family in prayer. A description of the expressions of prayer—vocal prayer, meditation, mental prayer (including contemplation)—serves as a prelude to a discussion of the struggle of prayer and the need to persevere in a spirit of love. All this is preliminary to the climax toward which the Catechism is leading: the study of the prayer most cherished by

Christians, the Lord's Prayer, which the second-century writer, Tertullian, called a "summary of the Gospel."

The Authority of the *Catechism*

While the Holy Father described the *Catechism* as "a sure norm for teaching the faith," it is important for us to realize as we read it that the statements it makes do not all have the same authority or importance. Statements from the councils of the Church have the highest authority, since they come from the highest teaching body in the Church, the pope and bishops gathered together in solemn assembly. Statements from individual Fathers of the Church or from various theologians have whatever authority these statements possessed before they were included in the *Catechism*.

This is not just my opinion; it is the position taken by the man whom Pope John Paul II charged to bring the *Catechism* to completion, Cardinal Joseph Ratzinger. In a seminar held on July 9, 1993, at Madrid in Spain, Cardinal Ratzinger said, "Every doctrinal point proposed by the *Catechism* has no authority but that which it already possesses."

The cardinal makes a very important point that we must keep in mind when reading the *Catechism*: It is not inclusion in this book that gives authority to a particular statement. Rather, as the cardinal makes clear, whatever authority they have belonged to them before they were inserted into the *Catechism*. Understanding the cardinal's principle will help us to see that not everything in the *Catechism* is of equal authority or importance. Catechists, especially, need to keep this in mind when they use it as a reference work.

Limitations and Shortcomings

We must realize that the *Catechism of the Catholic Church*, like any other catechism, has its limitations and shortcomings. Indeed, any and every human attempt to express in words God's self-revelation and our response to that revelation is bound to have imperfections and deficiencies, for the reality of God is too great for us ever to comprehend, much less to commit to writing. There is always more to learn. This means that there will always be positions once taken that have to be revised—even changed—in the light of further understandings of the truth. In John's Gospel Jesus promises his followers: "When the Spirit of Truth comes, he will guide you into all the truth" (John 16:13)—but he does not say "all at once." As Vatican II's *Constitution on Divine Revelation* tells us: "God, who spoke of old, still maintains an uninterrupted conversation with the bride of his beloved Son" (#8). This ongoing "conversation" of God with the Church influences the way the Church writes catechisms and other documents.

Does this mean that all catechisms are provisional documents that will always change with time? This cannot be answered with a simple yes or no. It must be firmly stated that there is nothing provisional about the substance of Catholic faith. Yet it must also be said, with equal firmness, that this substance will not always be expressed in the same way or even with the same clarity in different ages of the Church's history. Pope John XXIII, in his opening speech to the Second Vatican Council, made this point very forcefully: "The substance of the ancient deposit of faith is one thing; the way it is presented is another."

A catechism that comes to us from the magisterium of the Church will express the authentic teaching of the Church in accordance with the best understanding and conscience that the magisterium has at the time the catechism is produced. We who live in the last years of the twentieth century are able to say that, while the basic substance of the faith is essentially the same in the *Roman Catechism* of the Council of Trent and the *Catechism of the Catholic Church*, the way in which that substance is expressed in these two documents differs considerably. Both betray the times in which they were written. Most Catholics today will find the language of the new catechism much more congenial to them than the text of the *Roman Catechism*. The Tridentine catechism rose out of religious controversies that today are in large part foreign to us. The more ecumenical thrust of the new *Catechism* much better suits our present religious outlook.

If I were asked to point out the most striking contrast

between these two catechisms, I would choose Part Two in each of them, namely, the section that deals with the sacraments. Trent's catechism shows its indebtedness to the scholasticism that was the theological environment of the day. Thus, it presents the sacraments in terms of signs, matter and form, cause and effects, and so on. The *Catechism of the Catholic Church* begins its presentation of the sacraments with a fine study of liturgy and our participation in the celebration of the Christian mystery. It clearly reveals the influence of the twentieth-century liturgical movement and, influenced by that movement, Vatican II's *Constitution on the Sacred Liturgy*.

The *Catechism*'s emphasis on the social teachings of the Church and its linking of the Eucharist with concern for the poor is new. This is understandable: Those who wrote the *Roman Catechism* could not have known of the Industrial Revolution, the social ills that it bred and the Church's consequent obligation to speak out against the inhumanities that a technological society visits on so many people.

Many other examples of differences could be mentioned. Let one more issue—a highly emotional one—suffice: namely, the fate of children who die without Baptism. The Tridentine catechism is adamant: "Infants, unless baptized, cannot enter heaven" (page 24). The new *Catechism* speaks much more compassionately, saying that the Church simply entrusts children who have died without baptism to the mercy of God. The divine mercy and Jesus' tenderness toward children allow us to hope that there is a way of salvation for such children (see #1261).

Could the *Catechism of the Catholic Church* be improved upon? In several areas, I think. Readers would be better served by more attention to contemporary Scripture scholarship. More importantly, I miss that openness to the contemporary world's needs, questions and problems that characterized the documents of Vatican II, especially the *Pastoral Constitution on the Church in the Modern World*. While it clearly states the truth of the full humanity of Jesus, the *Catechism*'s emphasis on his divinity seems to leave little room for truly human knowledge in Jesus.

In yet another area, I would like to see a clearer expression of what precisely is the authority of the bishops in their local Churches, and of how those with authority in the Church can be enabled to listen more closely to the experience of people in the local Churches throughout the world: people of many different races, colors, cultures and ethnic backgrounds. I would have hoped, too, for greater recognition of creative thinking in the field of moral theology in many different parts of the world over the last twenty-five or thirty years.

About This Book

All this said, I am still convinced that this *Catechism* can serve a great need in the Church. It can be an especially worthwhile guide for catechists and parents in fulfilling their task of handing on the Church's faith. In this book, I shall strive to highlight important issues that are dealt with in the *Catechism.*

Given the size of the document, this book cannot do justice to the whole picture of Catholic faith presented there. I have tried to be faithful to the book's title, *Exploring the Catechism of the Catholic Church*; I have chosen to write about those areas most helpful for readers who want a brief but clear explanation of the basics of Catholic faith. I have tried sincerely to be true to the contents of the *Catechism* without attempting to follow its text slavishly. This means that, when it seemed appropriate, I arranged the material in an order of my own choosing rather than adhering strictly to the order of the *Catechism.*

The numbers appearing at various points refer to the articles of the Catechism. They are meant as a tool for the reader who might wish to read more fully what I have discussed only briefly and selectively.

Two sets of questions conclude each chapter. Growing in Knowledge questions test the reader's understanding of the chapter's contents. Growing in Faith questions encourage reflection on one's faith life.

To enliven the presentation, I have at times used illustrations and explanations of my own, something I think every catechist must do. These personal touches harmonize with the text and help to elucidate it, but the reader will not find them in the *Catechism*. In choosing the material for each chapter, I have tried to keep in mind the needs of the community of God's people at this time in the life of the Church. Others might well have chosen to emphasize other topics. I must, therefore, take personal responsibility for what is written in this book.

I shall be happy if this modest book opens doors into some of the major rooms of this huge edifice (the 803-page *Catechism of the Catholic Church*). I hope to shed some light on the faith that opens our hearts to God's self-communication, as we journey—often through darkness—toward the fullness of the Kingdom. There God will be all in all and we shall behold God face-to-face.

GROWING IN KNOWLEDGE

1) Why is the distinction between a universal catechism and a local catechism important?

2) What is the advantage of the catechism format? The danger?

3) What benefits does the new *Catechism* promise to you?

GROWING IN FAITH

1) Who had the most influence on your childhood religious education? Why do you name that person or persons?

2) Who or what influences your growth in faith now?

3) How are you a catechist? What has been your greatest challenge in passing on the faith?

4) Do you feel there is anything lacking in your understanding of the faith? What more do you want to know?

CHAPTER ONE

The God Whom Our Hearts Seek

> *And this is eternal life, that they may know you, the only true God, and Jesus Christ whom you have sent.*—John 17:3

The poet-preacher R. S. Thomas wrote:

> And one said
> speak to us of love
> and the preacher opened
> his mouth and the word *God*
> fell out....

For centuries people have wrestled over these two great mysteries: God and love. Indeed it may well be that they are the only mysteries worth grappling with. Some people have arrived at the awareness that the two cannot be separated. The disciple whom Jesus loved puts it simply and profoundly: "God is love" (1 John 4:16b). But many have not been able to make this identification. Catastrophic events like the Holocaust have moved some deeply religious people to assert that a God who could permit such devastation cannot be a God of love.

The Human Search for God (#28-30)

Like Jacob wrestling with the Unknown in the darkness of night, men and women through the centuries have wrestled with the question of God. Like Jacob they have dared to ask how to name God. But for all their pains, no completely satisfactory response has been forthcoming. They have received the same answer that Jacob did: "Why is it that you ask my name?" (Genesis 32:29b).

Part of the reason for this fascination with God is the fact that human beings are naturally religious; they instinctively search for meaning in life. If *God* is the word we use to describe the source of ultimate meaning, then it can be said that this very thirst to discover what life is all about indicates that people have a desire for God and some capacity to know about God.

Most people indulge this fascination in a fairly casual, haphazard way. But some in the human community go about the study of God in a planned and systematic way. The systematic study of God through reason, which has occupied the thoughts of distinguished men and women through the centuries, is part of what we know as philosophy. Saint Paul summed up the philosopher's approach as well as anyone when he wrote:

> For what can be known about God is plain to them, because God has shown it to them. Ever since the creation of the world his eternal power and divine nature, invisible though they are, have been understood and seen through the things he has made. (Romans 1:19-20)

Saint Augustine said much the same thing in his *Confessions*:

> Behold, the heavens and the earth *are*. They proclaim that they were made.... They also proclaim that they did not make themselves. "We are because we have been made; we did not exist before we existed, and therefore could not have made ourselves." (XI, 4)

The knowledge of God that philosophy achieves is valid and valuable, but ultimately unsatisfying to the human heart. For most of us it is not enough to find a God who answers the questions of our minds; we want a God to whom our hearts can respond. It is not just speculative talk about God that we want, but the experience of God. A God whose existence is known only as the result of intellectual argument can be kept at arm's length. A God who is experienced as present is a God who demands a response on our part.

In one of his unpublished journals, Thomas Merton wrote: "At the heart of philosophy is a secret 'nostalgia' for revelation." Merton himself is proof of that nostalgia. His quest for God took him, as it has many others, beneath the calm surface of reason to the dark waters below. He was not content to move on the surface, within easy reach of familiar shores. In his search for the deepest realms of reality, he had to become, as it were, a deep-sea diver reaching for the ocean bed. He had to go where reason alone could not take him.

God's Revelation

The supreme goodness of the divine heart has responded to that "nostalgia." God has made it possible for us to know and love our Creator in a way that far surpasses our natural capabilities. God has revealed the divine self to us and "made known to us the mystery of his will" (see Ephesians 1:9).

God's Saving Deeds (#50-63)

We must be clear about God's self-revelation. It did not occur through formulas or doctrinal statements, such as one might find in a book of theology or in a catechism. God spoke through deeds. God's creation of the world; God's call to Abraham to leave his own land and go to a place that God would show him; God's covenant-promise to Abraham that he would be the ancestor of a multitude of nations; God's deliverance of the Hebrews from slavery in Egypt and the gift at Mount Sinai of the covenant and the law: All these events that happened in human history are examples of divine actions. Through these actions God speaks to us. The "words" these actions speak reveal God as one who cares for a people, who liberates them from oppression and watches over them with solicitude and concern. God's deeds on behalf of this people are words of revelation spoken to us by God and telling us something of who God is.

God's Saving Words (#64)
But God also spoke through the prophets—people deeply sensitive to God's purposes. Sometimes eagerly (Isaiah, for instance), sometimes reluctantly (Jeremiah or Amos are both examples), these prophets called people to forsake their infidelities or suffer the terrible consequences. At the same time they held out the hope of a new and spectacular saving act of God, of a new and everlasting covenant, written in human hearts, that would be not just for a chosen people but for all the peoples of the earth.

Jesus, God's Final Revelation (#65-67)
And so, having revealed the divine self to us in saving deeds and in words spoken through chosen human instruments, God in the last days spoke to us through God's own Son. If past events of history had become words spoken by God, now in the fullness of time the very Word of God became an event occurring in history.

God's final revelation comes through God's eternal Word become one of us. In Jesus the Christ, the Word of God made flesh, God's self-revelation is complete. God has said everything. Jesus is God's last and everlasting Word. There can be no further revelation, for there is nothing more to reveal. Jesus says at the Last Supper: "When the Spirit of truth comes, he will guide you into *all the truth*.... [H]e will take what is mine and declare it to you. All that the Father has is mine. For this reason I said that he will take what is mine and declare it to you" (John 16:13a, 14b-15, emphasis added).

To say that there is nothing more to be revealed is not to deny that we have much to do in order to understand all that has been revealed. Through the centuries the Church has reflected on revelation; we continue to seek new meanings, deeper insight and clearer and more contemporary terminology.

If it is true to say that there is nothing more to be revealed, it is equally true to say that we shall never exhaust the meaning and intelligibility of what has been revealed. That is why it is possible to say that, while God's definitive revelation has been given and there is nothing to add to it, the dialogue between God and God's people continues through all of time.

The bishops said at Vatican II: "Thus God, who spoke in the past, continues to converse with the spouse of his beloved Son. And the Holy Spirit, through whom the living voice of the Gospel resounds in the Church—and through her in the world—leads believers to the full truth, and makes the Word of Christ dwell in them in all its richness."

The Transmission of God's Revelation (#74-83)

This full and final revelation of God was entrusted to the early Christian community. It was God's will that the revelation given for the salvation of all nations should be preserved in its integrity for all generations. This role, given first to the apostles, the chosen eyewitnesses of the Christ event, was handed on to the bishops and their successors. "This sacred Tradition ['handing on'], then, and the sacred Scripture of both Testaments are like a mirror in which the Church, during its pilgrim journey here on earth, contemplates God, from whom she receives everything, until such time as she is brought to see him face-to-face as he really is" (*Constitution On Divine Revelation*, #7).

Tradition and Scripture are closely related and cannot really be separated from one another because they both derive from the same divine source. Scripture and Tradition are handed down with authority by the successors of the apostles. At the same time we must understand that it is not only in the exercise of teaching that the Church hands on what it has received from the Lord. In its life and worship, as well as its teaching, the Church "perpetuates and transmits to every generation all that she herself is, all that she believes" and thus "is always advancing toward the plenitude of divine truth, until eventually the words of God are fulfilled in her" (*Constitution on Divine Revelation*, #8).

We Speak to God (#144)

God's words to us demand a response: a personal commitment of our whole selves to God as well as the adherence of our mind and heart to all that God says to us. It is a free human response to God's initiative and self-revelation. Genesis 12 gives us the first written description of a historical person with faith in God. Not that no one before Abraham had faith in God, but this is the first *record* we have of someone who has such faith. Faith, as revealed in the Abraham story, is the call to give up all that has offered security and to trust solely in God. Abraham is called to leave family and country and set out for an unknown destination. As the Letter to the Hebrews expresses it, "he set out, not knowing where he was going" (11:8b).

Faith, this story is telling us, is a journey in which we have no clear idea of the destination or the way to get there. But we have something greater: the consciousness that God is with us and that we make the journey at God's behest.

Faith, then is a relationship of commitment to God. For Israel it was to the God who delivered them from the slavery of Egypt; for Christians, it is to the God who raised Jesus from the dead. Faith is also a commitment to Jesus, "the beloved Son," in whom God was "well pleased," and to whom God ordered us to listen (see Mark 1:11; 9:7). Jesus himself said: "Believe in God, believe also in me" (John 14:1b). Finally, faith is a commitment to God's Spirit. As Paul says: "[N]o one comprehends what is truly God's except the Spirit of God" (1 Corinthians 2:11b). And elsewhere he writes that "no one can say 'Jesus is Lord' except by the Holy Spirit" (1 Corinthians 12:3).

We Believe... (#166)

Faith is a personal act, yet it is not an isolated act. We receive faith from others and, in turn, hand it on to others. Faith, therefore, is an ecclesial act: We receive faith from the Church, and it is the Church that sustains and nourishes our faith. We live faith in the daily realities of life. We celebrate it when we gather for worship. The sense of pride and joy we experience through our membership in the Christian faith community is beautifully expressed in the prayer of the Mass that precedes the Sign of Peace, when we ask the Lord Jesus to "look upon the faith of your Church."

Faith is the necessary context of prayer, whether liturgical prayer or personal prayer, whether prayer with words or wordless prayer. The whole person prays; still, Scripture regularly speaks of the heart as the source of prayer—and it must be a heart warmed by faith. In prayer faith enables us to discover our union with God. The life of prayer then becomes the awareness of being in the presence of God and in communion with God. Faith that comes to deep awareness of God is, therefore, a foretaste of that face-to-face vision of God which is the fulfillment of our journey into God.

The Content of Faith (#185-197)

The content of faith is set forth in the Church's creeds, especially the Apostle's Creed, which is a baptismal creed (hence it begins "I believe...") and the Nicene Creed, which is the community's profession of faith, particularly the liturgical community (and therefore begins "We believe..."). We conclude these creeds with "Amen"—a rousing yes, a final affirmation expressing our firm faith. The amen may serve, too, to remind us of Jesus who, to Saint Paul, was the Great Yes to God and to humanity. He was not, Paul says, alternately yes and no; he was never anything but yes (see 2 Corinthians 1:19).

The different articles of the Apostles' Creed occupy a long section in the *Catechism* (#185-1065). To study all of them in detail would require a whole book. I must be content with discussing some of them as we move all too rapidly through the pages of the *Catechism*. One general point I wish to make clear: The various creeds that have come into being through the course of history (for example, the Apostles' Creed, the Nicene Creed, the Athanasian Creed) do not exhaust the Church's expression of faith. As I pointed out above, Vatican II, in the document on Revelation, makes clear that the Church's life and liturgy also give expression to who it is and to what it believes.

The language we use to express faith is never adequate to express the realities we believe in. And it is the realities, not the doctrinal formulations, to which faith adheres. Nonetheless, the formulas of faith help us express what we believe, hand it on to others and celebrate our faith in the liturgical community.

We Speak About God (#39-49)

We know about God by reason. We can experience God

through revelation. But we can never express adequately in human words who God really is. The reality of God is too huge a burden for human language to bear. God is both transcendent and immanent. Transcendence means that God is not to be sought among the creatures God made. God's immanence means that God is not distant, but rather is in all reality as the Source from which it comes and the Ground of Being and Love in which it continues to exist. Thus, God is not infinitely remote, but close at hand. God is distinct from the world but not separate from it. Everything that is, is in God. Separated from the Ground that sustains it, it would simply cease to be.

The reason that we can name God at all is because the creatures God made reflect something of God's perfection, though only in an imperfect way. Thus we can note certain perfections in creatures and then say: "Yes, that perfection is in God." Thus we can talk about the wisdom we see in a highly intelligent friend and we can say: "God is wise." Yet we have to realize that wisdom in God is so much greater than wisdom in the creature that we can say with equal truth: "God is not wise (in the way that my friend is wise); for God's wisdom infinitely surpasses any and all human wisdom." Hence, when we talk about a perfection in creatures and then attribute it to God, we really have to say at the same time yes and no: God *is* this. God *is not* this.

Saint Thomas Aquinas said much the same thing when he wrote: "Concerning God, we cannot grasp what God is, but only what God is not, and how other beings stand in relation to God." The Fourth Lateran Council put it in this way: "Between the Creator and the creature there can be noted no similarity so great that a greater dissimilarity does not exist among them."

At the beginning of this chapter I spoke of John's words: "God is love." What John is doing in this remarkable statement is attributing to God a wonderful reality that we are able to experience in human relationships. How wonderful to realize that something we may have experienced very deeply in another person is but a faint shadow of that reality as it is in God. A faint shadow, because no one loves as God loves. How stupendous it is, then, to say that God *is* love!

God reveals the divine love to us through Jesus Christ, who is God incarnate come to save us, and in the Holy Spirit, who is God acting in our midst to further and complete the work of Jesus. In the very plan of salvation God reveals that the divine life is Trinitarian. Though it took the Church well into the fourth century before it arrived at a satisfactory (though necessarily inadequate) formulation of the doctrine of the Trinity, the mystery of God's Trinitarian relationship to us is clearly set forth in the Scriptures. Paul's prayer for the Corinthians (which is used in the Mass as an initial greeting) is Trinitarian: "The grace of the Lord Jesus Christ, the love of God, and the communion of the Holy Spirit be with all of you" (2 Corinthians 13:13).

The Trinity is the central mystery of faith, for it is both the source of all other mysteries and the light that helps to clarify them. At the same time it is at the very center of God's will to save the human race. As the *Catechism* puts it: "The whole history of salvation is identical with the history of the way and the means by which the one true God, Father, Son, and Holy Spirit, reveals himself...and reconciles and unites with himself those who turn away from sin" (#234).

How are we to deal with this awesome mystery? Of course we can, if we wish, simply make an act of faith. We can say: "I believe in the Trinity, but I really don't know what I'm talking about when I say the words." One could even muster up a good bit of enthusiasm about this kind of blind faith, as did the man who said of the Trinity: "Wish there were four of them, so that I could believe in more of them."

The Doctrine of the Trinity

But if we seek, as I suspect we do, more than blind faith in certain words, we will be wise to think in terms of the distinction made in the *Catechism* between the *mystery* of the Trinity and the *doctrine* of the Trinity. The mystery is about the inner life of God, revealed in God's dealings with us. The doctrine is the attempt we make, in words that are always woefully inadequate, to express the mystery.

In other words, we need to think of the Trinity at two levels. First, there is the level of the words which make up the doctrine. It took centuries to come up with those words. But we must never forget that whatever we do to put into words what we mean when we say "Blessed" and "Trinity," our efforts always fall far, far short of the reality. It isn't just that we cannot say it all. It's that we can say practically nothing that really tells us what we mean when we pronounce the words: "Blessed Trinity." The words clarify the *doctrine*. They cannot fully convey the *mystery*.

Beyond this level of words that try to articulate the doctrine, there is a second and much deeper level: namely, the inner life of God that the doctrine is intended to embody. When we come to this level, there is only one appropriate attitude: silence and contemplation. We can express the doctrine; we cannot adequately describe God's inner life.

Where does the doctrine of the "Blessed Trinity" come from? It comes from reflection on what Scripture has to say about God and what we as Christian women and men are able to say about how God relates to us. For while we cannot know the intimate life of God, we can reflect on what we are told about God in Scripture. We can also reflect on the ways in which God's saving actions touch us in our lives.

The doctrine of the Trinity, therefore, tells us two things: (1) how God relates to us as God works out the salvation of people in history, and (2) something of what we can know about the inner life of God. But it should be clearly understood that we know the latter only because we know the former.

The *Catechism* points out a distinction made by the Greek Fathers between "theology" (*theologia*) and "economy" (*oikonomia*). Don't be put off by these words, for they are helpful in understanding how important the Trinity is to our living of the Christian life. *Theology*, in this context, refers to the mystery of God's inmost life as Trinity (one God, three persons). *Economy*, as used here, has nothing to do with finances. It contains the Greek work *oikos*, which means "house." Literally, it means the "management of the affairs of a household." In reference to the Trinity, *economy* may be understood as referring to "the way in which God has managed the salvation of the household of the faith." In other words, the word speaks of the Trinity as we come to know it in God's plan of salvation, which unfolds in human history. The economy of salvation, therefore, refers to all the works by which God reveals the divine Self and communicates divine life to people.

Since God so loved the world as to send the Son, we come to know Father and Son. Since Jesus, before his passion, promised to send the Spirit to be with his disciples after Jesus' glorification in order to bring them all into the truth and to complete the work begun by Jesus, we come to know of the Holy Spirit.

Knowing the ways in which God relates to us helps us to understand, however inadequately, the mystery of God's inmost being. Think of it in this way. We come to know human beings through their actions; at the same time, knowing them helps us to understand the way they act. The "economic Trinity" (God's actions in human history) reveals the "theology" of the Trinity (God's very self); in turn, that theology sheds light on the economy of salvation.

One God, Three Persons (#253-256)

The Trinity, the *Catechism* says, is one. Christianity is monotheistic. We do not confess three Gods, but one God in three Persons. It is not that they share divinity, each being part; rather each is God whole and entire.

Yet, while the three Persons are one, they are really distinct from one another. As the sixth-century Council of Toledo (Spain, not Ohio) expressed it: "He is not the Father who is the Son, nor is the Son he who is the Father, nor is the Holy Spirit he who is the Father or the Son" (quoted in the *Catechism*, #254). Thus, the divine Persons, while unique, are not solitary. They are one in *what* they are; they are three in *who* they are.

Persons and Relations (#253-256)

For when we talk about three persons in one God, we are talking about relations. There are three distinct relations. Or, if you will, the Father is Father precisely because he is related to the Son as the One who gives to the Son the totality of what he *is* as Father except being Father. The Son is Son precisely because he is the One who has received all that the Son is. The Spirit is Spirit because the Spirit is the subsistent relationship of love between Father and Son as they give themselves to one another. *There is total oneness in what they are*; yet, also, three distinct relations. Or, if you will, there are three Persons perfectly related, whom we call Father, Son and Spirit, who are one God. As Gregory of Nazianzus expressed it so poetically: "Each Person considered in himself is entirely God.... I have not even begun to think of unity when the Trinity bathes me in its splendor. I have not even begun to think of the Trinity when unity grasps me" (quoted in #256).

The wondrous thing about this seemingly heavy scholastic approach is that catching a glimpse of this divine Community in which each possesses totally all that the others are, offers us a model for understanding what human community can and should mean. We come to see that it is not in separating ourselves from others that we find our identity. Quite the opposite: it is by identifying ourselves with others—by sharing as fully as we can all that we are—that we find our uniqueness and our personal identity.

To put it simply, it is in relationship that I discover who I am. It is in relating to others in the context of community that I am able to become the person I am called to be. In fact, relationship is so important to being human that, if you could conceive of the possibility of someone existing but having absolutely no relationships, that one, I think, would scarcely be a person. What makes me fully human is being joined to others in a network of relationships that makes us one.

The doctrine of the Trinity, then, need not be thought of as something to be left in dusty theological books. It has a unique significance for us. It can help us to understand a profoundly human problem: namely how we relate solitude (something we all need as persons) to community (something we all need for our fulfillment).

But most of all, the doctrine of the Trinity helps us to understand the plan God had in mind from the beginning of time: uniting all of us to God. As the *Catechism* puts it: "The ultimate end of the whole divine economy is the entry of God's creatures into the perfect unity of the Blessed Trinity" (#260).

In fact, we are already dwelling places of the Trinity, for Jesus says, "Those who love me will keep my word, and my Father will love them, and we will come to them and make our home with them" (John 14:23, quoted in #260).

GROWING IN KNOWLEDGE

1) What is the difference between saying, "There is nothing more to be revealed," and "Our awareness of God's revelation is ever-growing"?

2) What roles does the Church play in God's revelation?

3) How is God transcendent? How is God immanent?

4) How can faith be both personal and communal?

5) What is the purpose of prayer?

GROWING IN FAITH

1) What experience in your life resembles Jacob's "wrestling with God" in Genesis 32:24-29?

2) Is your knowledge of God more "head knowledge" or "heart knowledge"? How well can the two be separated?

3) How have you experienced the "saving hand of God" in your life? What was the effect on your faith?

4) With what kind of prayer are you most comfortable?

CHAPTER TWO

Jesus Christ, Son of God

If he were not true God, he would not be able to bring us healing; if he were not true man, he would not be able to give us an example.—Saint Leo the Great

"Honk if you love Jesus" said the bumper sticker popular some years ago. It invited people to express their love for Jesus in a way that is hardly demanding. The Gospels call for much more: Keep my commandments, if you love me; feed my lambs and my sheep if you love me; deny your very self, take up your cross and come after me if you love me. Honking one's horn may well be a gesture of love for Jesus. But true discipleship calls for more than gestures. It demands total commitment to him and to living out all he taught. No other human being who walked the face of the earth could make such demands.

Who Is Jesus? (#571-667)

Who is this Jesus who presumes to demand nothing less than everything from us? Jesus of Nazareth is the son of Mary, born in Bethlehem of Judah in the time of King Herod during the reign of the Emperor Caesar Augustus. He was a carpenter by trade. He lived most of his life in obscurity. For a short period of three years or so, he went about preaching God and God's coming reign. His teachings, especially what he had to say about God and God's love for sinners and outcasts, roused opposition. He was brought to trial and put to death at the order of Pontius Pilate, the Roman procurator in Judea from A.D. 26 to 36 (#423).

If that were all we could say about him, it would be difficult to justify the unconditional demands he makes on us. But there is more: He did not stay dead. On the third day God raised him from the dead. His tomb was empty and he appeared to many of his followers. These followers, inspired by a Spirit they had never experienced before, began preaching that God had raised Jesus from the dead and that in him a new creation had begun.

God had vindicated Jesus' teaching. But more than that, in Jesus God had reconciled the human family to God. In Jesus God revealed the divine love for us. In Jesus God enabled us to participate in the divine nature. In Jesus God offered us a model of true humanity and holiness.

The Human Heart of God (#464-483)

But what I have said thus far still does not reveal the full story. It does not go to the heart of the mystery of Jesus. For Jesus is not only the true son of Mary and a carpenter by trade, rabbi and teacher and victim of oppression. Unique of all human children, Jesus is the one in whom the fullness of God dwells bodily (see Colossians 2:9). Jesus of Nazareth is nothing less than the Son of God, begotten of the Father from all eternity.

This mystery of the utter uniqueness of Jesus we call the Incarnation. *The Son of God became one of us that we might become one with him.* In the soaring Prologue of the Fourth Gospel, John calls Jesus God's Word (that is, God's full revelation) and tells us that the Word was made flesh and lived among us—literally, "he pitched his tent in our midst." This striking image has roots in the Hebrew Scriptures, our Old Testament. During the Israelites' sojourn in the desert after their escape from Egypt, they lived in tents. One tent, the tent of the Holy Presence, contained the Ark of the Covenant. It was God's tent in the midst of God's people. What the Fourth Gospel tells us is that God has pitched a tent in the midst of the whole human race. In Jesus God has become human. God loves us with a human heart.

True God and True Man (#464-470)

The Incarnation embodies a great mystery. Jesus is at once divine and human. What he was (God) he remained, and what he was not (human) he assumed. We cannot accept one element of the mystery and ignore the other. We must accept both at white heat. Jesus was not just adopted by God; he was and is God. At the same time, his humanity was not absorbed into his divinity. He is fully human, just as he is fully divine. Being human, Jesus was limited: He was born at a certain time and in a certain place. He learned in a human way.

The puzzle, which we can state but not resolve, is this: How could Jesus learn humanly what he already knew divinely? We cannot exactly answer this. All we can say is that, if he was truly human, then the normal qualities that go with being human (except sin) must have belonged to him. His humanity was not an act. He must truly have learned and grown in knowledge. When he asked "Who touched me?" (see Luke 8:45), it makes sense to say that he was truly looking for information that as a man he did not have.

The *Catechism* speaks of Jesus as growing in wisdom, stature and grace, and then adds that he would even have to gain for himself what can be learned only from experience (#472). Was there some kind of difference between his human experience and ours? The *Catechism* unquestionably asserts the full humanity of Jesus.

In Mark 13:32 Jesus speaks of the end of the world: "But about that day or hour no one knows, neither the angels in heaven, nor the Son, but only the Father." The *Catechism* clearly refers to this statement: "By its union to the divine wisdom in the person of the Word incarnate, Christ enjoyed in his human knowledge the fullness of understanding of the eternal plans he had come to reveal. What he admitted to not knowing in this area, he elsewhere declared himself not sent to reveal" (#474).

Does this statement seem to be saying that, at least as far as knowing God's plan is concerned, the divine wisdom so "invaded" the human intellect of Christ that it could not, or at least need not, operate in a normal human way? In other words, that he knew the divine plan humanly without having to learn it in a human way?

This seems to be the intent; yet it is a fact that the *Catechism* also quotes more than once Hebrews 4:15: "For we do not have a high priest who is unable to sympathize with our weaknesses, but we have one who in every respect has been tested as we are, yet without sin." One of our human weaknesses is ignorance of certain things, including the details of God's redemptive plan (#540). Perhaps the best we can say is that, in discussing the question of the human knowledge of Jesus, the *Catechism* is obviously struggling with mystery—and so must we.

Scriptural Names for Jesus (#430-451)

Jesus. Jesus (in Hebrew *Joshua*, in Greek, *Jesous*) means "The Lord [*Yahweh*] saves." In Matthew 1:21, Joseph is told to give this name to the son Mary has conceived by the Holy Spirit because "he will save his people from their sins." Jesus is his *proper* name. In his own person, Jesus brings the very name of God into the history of humankind. There is, Peter tells the early Christian community, "no other name under heaven given among mortals by which we must be saved" (Acts 4:12). This name dear to his followers is at the center of Christian prayer. Liturgical prayers are concluded "through our Lord Jesus Christ...." This name is the climax of the Hail Mary. In the Eastern Church it is the prayer of the heart, repeated over and over again: "Lord, Jesus Christ, Son of God, have mercy on me, a sinner."

Christ. Equivalent of the Hebrew *Messiah*, "Christ" is not Jesus' surname but his *title*, which means "anointed." In the Old Testament kings, priests and occasionally prophets were anointed. "Anointed" meant being consecrated to the task received from God. Jesus was anointed by his very birth, and in a special way at his baptism, to be God's unique instrument of salvation. Because many of the people of his time thought of the Messiah as an earthly ruler who would fulfill the Jewish people's nationalistic expectations, Jesus avoided using the term and ordered others not to use it. Only after the resurrection was Peter able to proclaim Jesus' true kingship: "...[L]et the entire house of Israel know with certainty that God has made him both Lord and Messiah [Christ], this Jesus whom you crucified" (Acts 2:36).

Only Son of God. In the Old Testament "Son of God" was

applied to the people of Israel and to their kings. It did not imply divinity, but rather an adoption by God that created a special intimacy with God. But the disciples' post-resurrection statements clearly and certainly meant divinity. Thus Paul writes that Jesus "was declared to be Son of God with power according to the spirit of holiness by resurrection from the dead" (Romans 1:4). And the Fourth Gospel tells us: "We have seen his glory, the glory as of a father's only son, full of grace and truth" (John 1:14b).

Lord. In the very important third chapter of *Exodus*, God accedes to Moses' request and gives him the divine name. This name is made up of four Hebrew consonants—in English, YHWH—whose pronunciation and meaning has been lost. We pronounce it "Yahweh," but that is little more than a guess. It has been taken to mean "I AM WHO I AM." Whatever its meaning and pronunciation, it is the proper name of God.

When the Hebrew Scriptures were translated into Greek two centuries before Christ, the name *YHWH* was rendered *Kyrios*, "Lord" (as in *Kyrie eléison,* "Lord, have mercy"). Thewword was, therefore, the strongest way of asserting the true divinity of Israel's God, for it is the Greek equivalent of God's very name.

When Paul speaks of the reward God gave to Jesus for humbling himself even to death on a cross in that moving hymn in Philippians, he says: "Therefore God also highly/exalted him/and gave him the name/that is above every name" (Philippians 2:9). The name above every name is, of course, the name *Kyrios*, "Lord." Thus the New Testament uses the word *Lord* to refer to God; but what is new is that it also uses that name to designate Jesus. It expresses his risen splendor: Because of his victory over death, he is supreme Lord of life and death. The divine name proclaims his divine sovereignty.

In our prayer we sometimes invoke the Father as Lord; at other times we use "Lord" to mean the risen Jesus. Thus, we conclude our prayer "through Christ our Lord." Three times we invoke Jesus as our healing savior when, in the Penitential Rite of the Mass, we pray: "Lord, have mercy; Christ, have mercy; Lord, have mercy."

When the Church came into contact with the Roman Empire

in the first century of its existence, it met a world where Caesar was lord. As a countercultural movement in the ancient world, at the price of martyrdom, Christians insisted that people must not submit their personal freedom to any earthly power, but only to God and to God's Christ. Caesar is not lord; Jesus is. Indeed, the earliest Christian profession of faith was the simplest of all our creeds: "Jesus is Lord." Such profession of faith demanded the grace of the Holy Spirit. Paul insists that "no one can say 'Jesus is Lord' except by the Holy Spirit" (1 Corinthians 12:3c). The very last words of the New Testament express the longing of Christians for final completion of the divine plan of salvation that the Lord's return will accomplish. Hence the cry that closes the book of *Revelation*: "Amen. Come, Lord Jesus!" (Revelation 22:20b).

The Mysteries of Christ (#512-521)

The two great mysteries of the life of Jesus are the Incarnation (his becoming one of us) and the Paschal Mystery (his death, resurrection and ascension). When we speak of the mysteries of the rosary, we speak of various events that center around one or other of these principal mysteries. But there is also a sense in which all the events of Jesus' life were mysteries. They teach us. They reveal God to us. They are saving realities for us.

Jesus' Public Ministry (#574-574)

During the greater part of his life, Jesus shared the condition of the vast majority of human beings: a largely uneventful life filled with manual labor. The relatively short time of his public ministry followed immediately on the ministry of John the Baptist. Jesus' message seemed to be in continuity with John's. They began their preaching with the same call: "Repent, for the kingdom of heaven has come near" (Matthew 3:2; 4:17b). It is as if John begins something that Jesus will bring to completion.

Yet there is a fundamental discontinuity between Jesus and John that points up the newness of Jesus' message. Both call people to repentance in view of the coming Kingdom. But John is in essential continuity with Amos, Jeremiah and the rest of the prophets. His message is: Repent or else. Repent, for God's wrath is about to strike. Jesus breaks with this prophetic thrust. Like the prophets he calls people to repentance in view of God's inbreaking into the world. But Jesus' sense of that inbreaking is different from that of the prophets. His message is utterly new: "Repent because God is about to save you. Repent and believe in the good news" (#541).

The Kingdom (#543-544). The Kingdom Jesus proclaims is for all who accept the word of God, especially for the poor and the lowly, the "little ones" to whom God has revealed the mysteries that remain hidden to the wise and the great. One of the distinctive features of Jesus' preaching of the Kingdom is the call extended to sinners—not only in a general way but to particular individuals: the sinful woman, the tax-collector Zacchaeus and so many others. In Jesus' dealings with people the compassion of God became a visible reality in our world.

The Parables. Jesus frequently taught through parables, stories taken from ordinary life-events. Their purpose was not to point to a moral, but to call people to make a radical decision for God. It would be a mistake to read the parables as announcements of eternal moral principles. They are intended to challenge the hearer: "What ought I to do? What would a disciple of Jesus do in this sort of situation?"

The Miracles. Though Jesus performed miracles out of compassion, he made no effort to call attention to them. Nor did he cure everyone who was ill. The miracles were not apologetic tools to convince people that he was from God. They were rather signs (the word used by the Fourth Gospel to describe them) of the inbreaking of the Kingdom of God into the world. Often it was faith that called forth the miracle; always faith was strengthened by the miracle. The miracles were signs that the Messianic Son of God had come to liberate people from the slavery of sin, which destroys our freedom and reduces us to bondage. In Jesus the healing power of God was acting to rejuvenate people in body and spirit.

Jesus' Paschal Mystery: Death and Resurrection (#571-679)

Though Jesus initially won great crowds by his preaching, he also upset Israel's religious authorities by his attitude toward the Law and the Temple, and by the vision of God he proclaimed in his preaching. They were especially scandalized when he identified his own merciful attitude toward sinners with God's attitude toward them. One has only to read the three great parables of Luke 15 (The Lost Sheep, The Lost Coin and The Prodigal Son) to see how Jesus defines God in terms of unconditional love. Jesus' identification of himself with God. "The Father and I are one" (John 10:30), was too much for them to stomach. They had him brought to Pilate for trial.

The historical details surrounding his trial are complex and confusing. Only God can judge the personal guilt of those actually involved in the trial and the events that led up to it. Certainly it is wrong and cruel to impute guilt to a whole nation for the trial and death of Jesus.

Death as Redemptive Love

The Gospel writers see Jesus' death as redemptive. It fulfilled Isaiah's prophecy about the Suffering Servant. Details of the Passion are often described in words reminiscent of the Isaian Servant: "The righteous one, my servant, shall make many righteous,/and he shall bear their iniquities" (Isaiah 53:11).

The death of Jesus is a revelation of love: God's love and Jesus' love. "For God so loved the world that he gave his only Son so that everyone who believes in him may not perish but may have eternal life" (John 3:16, 17b). His death also reveals Jesus' love for us: "...Christ loved us and gave himself up for us, a fragrant offering and sacrifice to God" (Ephesians 5:2b).

By raising Jesus from the dead, God placed the divine seal of approval on all that Jesus had said and done. Without the Resurrection, joined to Jesus' death, we would not be saved. We would still be in our sins. As Paul says: "...[I]f Christ has not been raised, then our proclamation has been in vain and your faith has been in vain" (1 Corinthians 15:14).

The death and resurrection of Jesus meant the beginning of a new creation. Humanity, estranged from God by sin, was reconciled to God through the blood of Christ poured out for the forgiveness of sins. As Paul expresses it: "So if anyone is in Christ, there is a new creation: everything old has passed away; see, everything has become new! All this is from God, who reconciled us to himself...; that is, in Christ God was reconciling the world to himself" (2 Corinthians 5:17-18a, 19a).

Thus, the Paschal Mystery involves not just the death of Jesus, but also his Resurrection. They are not two separate realities but two sides of the same reality. As we proclaim at liturgy, dying he destroyed our death; rising he restored our life. The Resurrection, following on Jesus' death, is the door to new life both for Jesus and for us.

The angel's announcement at the tomb, "He has been raised" (Mark 16:6b), describes an event unlike any other in human history. Every other event takes place and then is swallowed up in the past. The Resurrection of Jesus is a once-and-for-all event. It is the one event that is contemporary with every age of history.

The Resurrection was not mere resuscitation. That had happened before: Jesus had brought Lazarus and the widow of Naim's son back to life—resuscitated them for a time. But because they came back to the same kind of mortal life they had lived before, they would die again.

Resurrection was something totally new. It was not a coming back from the dead, but a going *beyond* death and entering into an entirely new kind of existence, an immortal existence. The Risen One has gone beyond time and space. Yet at the same time he is everywhere; he belongs to all history and to all peoples. He is in our midst.

But more than that: He enables us to participate in the new creation. Jesus the Christ is the "firstborn of all creation," the "firstborn from the dead" (Colossians 1:15b, 18b), "the firstborn within a large family" (Romans 8:29b). By Baptism we are incorporated into the Paschal Mystery of the Lord Jesus. We live in our daily lives its rhythm of dying and rising. We celebrate it in the Eucharist. When we die we die into the fullness of the new life Christ has gained for us. Death has been robbed of its victory; it is no longer loss but gain. For in death

Jesus brings us back to our beginning: to God.

This is what Paul is saying in the majestic passage in 1 Corinthians where he tells us that in the end God will subject all things, even death, to Christ. Then Paul orchestrates a soaring climax: When, finally, all has been subjected to him, "then the Son himself will also be subjected to the one who put all things in subjection under him, so that God may be all in all" (1 Corinthians 15:28).

GROWING IN KNOWLEDGE

1) In what ways are Jesus' "hidden years" a model for today's families and workers?

2) What does it mean to say that Jesus was fully human? Fully divine?

3) Why do we have so many names or titles for Jesus?

4) How is Jesus strikingly different from the prophets?

5) Why are the death and resurrection of Jesus two sides of the same reality?

GROWING IN FAITH

1) What does it mean to you that Jesus lived most of his life in obscurity?

2) Imagine God making up names for you. What might they be?

3) In what ways do we name other "lords" besides Jesus?

4) What does Jesus' resurrection mean to you? Can you identify any "resurrection experiences" in your life?

CHAPTER THREE

What Is the Church?

The Church has no other light than Christ's; according to a favorite image of the Church Fathers, the Church is like the moon, all its light reflected from the sun.—Catechism of the Catholic Church, #748

Married couples enjoy going out on occasion to celebrate an anniversary or a birthday or Valentine's Day. Such celebrations bring back happy memories: perhaps their first date, the day they became engaged or their wedding day. They may ask the band or orchestra to play "their song," some song associated with a special moment of tenderness and growth in their relationship. Hearing it brings back the thrill of that precious past moment.

An Easter People

This chapter is about the Church. To some, *Church* may designate a reality that seems impersonal, remote, outside of them. But to those who understand what Church really is, the word evokes sentiments similar to those associated with an anniversary or Valentine's Day or "our song." For the Church is not something outside us; rather it has to do with a unique relationship to God that we have as a people. It is a love relationship in which God loves us first and enables us to love God and our sisters and brothers in return. It is a relationship quite capable of evoking sentiments of tenderness and endearment.

Saint Augustine said it as well as anyone when he described

the Christian community in these words: "We are Easter people and 'alleluia' is our song." It is the Easter experience, first of Jesus and then of ourselves in him, that makes us the kind of lovers we are. And it is in the Easter experience that we hear our song.

So central is the Easter experience for us and so appropriate is our "alleluia" that during the Lenten season, as we prepare for a renewed experience of the Easter reality, we give up our song for forty days. This is a kind of dramatic symbol that, because of our sinfulness and selfishness, part of us has died; we have to go through a period of reconciliation and renewal. Then on Easter that part of us which was dead comes to life. Once again we feel free to sing our song. We discover anew our identity as Easter people.

When we speak of the Church, therefore, we need to keep in mind that we are talking about something deeply personal. First and foremost, we are talking about people, about ourselves: people gathered together by the risen Jesus to celebrate his presence among us and to continue his mission in the world. The *Catechism* has some memorable words describing the Church and its relationship to Christ and to his Spirit. It is "like the moon, all its light reflected from the sun," the risen Jesus. Or again: The Church is the place "where the Spirit flourishes" in the midst of God's people.

Different Meanings of Church (#751-776; #781-786)

The word *Church* (in Latin *ecclesia* from the Greek *ek-kalein*, "to call together") means a "gathering of people," "an assembly called together by God." In the Greek Old Testament, it was used to describe the people of Israel. It applied to them most especially when they assembled at Mount Sinai to receive the Law and to be constituted as God's holy people.

In Christian usage, apart from designating a building, *Church* has three different but closely connected meanings. It may mean the *local or particular community* (the diocese). It is in the local community that people experience the reality of being Church. Here they are baptized. Here they celebrate the Eucharist, Reconciliation and the whole sacramental life of the Church. Here they are involved in a mission to share the gospel with those who have it not.

Church also means the *universal community* of believers. More than a mere federation of Churches, this means the local or particular Churches in communion with one another and, most importantly, in communion with that local Church that is the center of Catholic unity: the Roman Church, which, in the phrase of Ignatius of Antioch, "presides in love."

Finally, *Church* is used to designate *the liturgical* (especially the eucharistic) *assembly*. The Church is most fully itself as it shares the meal and offers with Christ the sacrifice which reconciles us with God.

God's Plan

The Church is the gradual working out of God's plan for the restoration of all people to communion with God. Foreshadowed in creation, it found expression in the different covenants God made: with Noah, Abraham and, especially, Israel. In the fullness of time God's Son came to begin moving the divine plan toward its fulfillment. Jesus preached not the Church, but the Kingdom. But he laid the foundations of the Church as the beginning of the Kingdom. In the Church, then, the Kingdom is already present in a mysterious but imperfect way.

The laying of the Church's foundation is seen above all in Jesus' choice of the Twelve with Peter as their head, and in his celebration of a new covenant meal with them. The Spirit of God, sent by the risen Jesus, reveals the Church on Pentecost.

The Church as Mystery of Faith (#770-776)

In opening the second session of the Second Vatican Council in 1963, Pope Paul VI said: "The Church is a mystery...ever susceptible of newer and deeper investigation." This means that the Church cannot be described adequately in a hasty definition. It is like a precious jewel that must be looked at from many different angles. It is the People of God, the Body of Christ, the Bride of Christ, the Temple of the Holy Spirit. All these metaphors help to shed light on the reality of Church. Yet neither a single image nor all the images taken together can exhaust the meaningfulness of the Church.

The Church is mystery in another sense. The Greek word for "mystery" is often used as the equivalent of sacrament. A sacrament is a visible sign of God's presence and action in the world. Christ, because he is precisely *that*, is the Great Sacrament. The Church is the visible post-Resurrection sign (sacrament) of Christ's presence among his people, leading them to holiness of life and toward the fullness of the Kingdom. The Church, then, is the sacrament of universal salvation, the sign and instrument of communion between God and humanity.

The seven sacraments, which the Eastern Churches call the "sacred mysteries," are Christ's saving actions enacted among the people of God that make them into "a chosen race, a royal priesthood, a holy nation, God's own people" (1 Peter 2:9a).

The Church as the Body of Christ (#787-807)

There is an inexpressible oneness of life in the Church that comes from Christ through his Spirit and flows to all the members. Jesus describes his union with them as the union of the vine with its branches: They receive life from him. It was Paul who used the beautiful image of the Body of Christ to express the union between Christ and his disciples.

This unity does not take away the diversity of gifts. The Preface for Christian Unity prays:

> How wonderful are the works of the Spirit,
> revealed in so many gifts!
> Yet how marvelous is the unity
> the Spirit creates from their diversity,
> as he dwells in the hearts of your children....

The Holy Spirit works in many ways to build up the whole Body of Christ in love. Let us count the ways: *Baptism*, which incorporates us into the Body; the *other sacraments*, which bring growth and healing; the grace of the *apostles*, which holds first place among the Spirit's gifts; the *virtues* which order our actions toward the good of the whole Body, especially toward those who suffer: the poor, the afflicted and the oppressed; and finally, the *various charisms* that empower the baptized to undertake functions and tasks that contribute to the Church's renewal and growth, to the good of the human race, to the needs of all the world.

These charisms, as Pope John Paul said in an audience on June 24, 1992, enable us to realize that "the universal priesthood of the ecclesial community is led by the Spirit with a sovereign freedom that is amazing." He points out that not infrequently in the course of history, many of the faithful and above all the saints "have given popes and other pastors the light and strength necessary for fulfilling their mission, especially at difficult times for the Church."

The Church: One Holy, Catholic, Apostolic (#811-945)

The redemptive act of Christ tore down the barriers that separated people from one another. As Paul wrote to the Galatians: "There is no longer Jew or Greek, there is no longer slave or free, there is no longer male and female; for all of you are one in Christ Jesus" (3:28). Hence the Church is one.

The Church Is One

What are the bonds of unity that join us together? First of all is the inner bond of love, which "binds everything together in perfect harmony" (Colossians 3:14b). There are also visible bonds: the profession of one faith handed down from the apostles, the common celebration of the sacraments, the apostolic succession of the ordained ministry.

Yet, sadly, we realize that even though Christ broke down the barriers of separation, people throughout history have erected new ones. Love is not always there to bind people together. Almost from the very beginning, divisions have arisen in the Church. These divisions, rooted in the past, affect many today, even though they are not responsible for the divisions.

Ecumenism (#820-822). An important movement of our time is ecumenism, which seeks to restore unity among separated Christians. It is actually a twentieth-century phenomenon to which the Roman Catholic Church has come only in the last half of the century. Not till the 1950s did we acknowledge other Christians as "separated brethren" (the phrase is Pius XII's); not till the Second Vatican Council did we accept other denominations as constituting Churches of Christ. The *Constitution on the Church* stated that "the one Church of Christ...abides [*subsistit*] in the Catholic Church, governed by Peter's successor and the bishops in communion with him." "Abides in" (rather than "is") is clarified by the assertion that "many elements of sanctification and truth" exist beyond the visible bonds of the Catholic Church: "God's written word; the life of grace; faith, hope and love, together with other gifts of the Holy Spirit as well as visible elements." This means that the Holy Spirit may make use of these Churches as a means of salvation and a way to call us all back to full unity.

Jesus' prayer for his disciples was and continues to be "that they may all be one. As you, Father, are in me and I am in you, may they also be [one] in us, so that the world may believe that you have sent me" (John 17:21). As the *Catechism* says: The movement to recover the unity of all Christians is Christ's gift and the Spirit's call (see #820).

While unity is a gift that we cannot achieve by ourselves, but only through the grace of Christ's Spirit, there is much we can do to help build unity. There must be repentance for the infidelities of the past that have caused division. There must be ongoing renewal and conversion of heart. We must know well our own tradition and be willing to learn about the traditions of others. We need to listen to one another on both sides of the ecumenical fence. (How different another person's position appears when he or she explains it than when we try to express it on our words!) Above all, we must pray together and work together to overcome the oppression, the prejudice, the injustice that exist in our world. We must cooperate in the mutual task of achieving justice, nonviolence and peace.

The Church Is Holy

As we look over the Church's history, practically from the beginning we see much that can be deplored, much need for reform, renewal and repentance. It may be that the word *holy* does not come readily to our lips when we think of the Church. Yet we must not forget that the Church is united with Christ, God's Holy One. From him it has the means of becoming holy and in him has a model of true holiness. Moreover, the Church's only professed goal is to bring holiness to all its members and thus to give glory to God.

Saint Paul did not hesitate to address the people of the various Churches he founded as "saints"; yet no one knew better than he that most of them were far from perfect. As members of the Church baptized into Christ, we are saints, we are holy. But we are holy somewhat in the same sense as we are human. There is much in us that is less than human and we have to grow into the fullness of true humanity. In a similar way, there is much in us that does not conform to the model given us in Christ; still we strive to grow into the likeness of Christ. As Paul puts it: "But speaking the truth in love, we must grow up in every way into him who is the head, into Christ..." (Ephesians 4:15). The wheat and the weeds grow together in the Church and in each of us. The Church, therefore, is at once holy and yet ever in need of reform and purification.

The Church Is Catholic

Catholic means having wholeness, universality. The Church is catholic because it has Christ and the means of salvation he offers to all peoples. It is catholic also in its mission, for all human beings are called to belong to the new people of God under the headship of Christ. As the Vatican II *Constitution on the Church* says: "The note of universality characterizing the people of God is the Lord's gift by which the Catholic Church efficaciously and perpetually strives to recapitulate all humanity, with all its riches, under Christ the head in the unity of his Spirit" (#13).

Universality is wondrously expressed in the rich variety of Church disciplines, liturgical rites and theological and spiritual heritages that spring from the different cultural and social backgrounds proper to the many local Churches throughout the world.

The Church, in its concern to be catholic, recognizes its

bonds with those who have not accepted the gospel. It is linked with the Jewish people, "the first to hear the Word of God," as we pray in the Good Friday liturgy; to the people of Islam, who profess fidelity to the faith of Abraham and adore the one merciful God; and to all people of goodwill who search for the unknown God, the Source and Sustainer of life who wills to bring all peoples to salvation. While the Church has the mission to preach the gospel to all nations, it has also the responsibility to enter into respectful dialogue with those who do not accept it. Such dialogue enables those who proclaim the gospel to see the wondrous (if sometimes hidden) operations of God's grace among all peoples.

The Church Is Apostolic

The Church is apostolic in that it was founded on the apostles and has preserved, through the protecting grace of the Holy Spirit, the teachings handed down from their time. The apostolic nature of the Church continues because of apostolic succession. "Apostolic succession" means that the college of bishops of the Church united with the Bishop of Rome, the successor of Peter, carry on by divine right the mission Jesus entrusted to the apostles.

The office of the apostles was unique and unrepeatable. They were to proclaim the gospel as the chosen companions of Jesus during his ministry and especially as witnesses to the Resurrection. But there is an enduring aspect to their office, since Christ promised to remain with them all days, even to the end of the world (see Matthew 28:20). That is why the apostles took care to appoint successors. The bishops are the successors of the apostles, as the Bishop of Rome is the successor of Peter, whom Jesus placed at the head of the apostolic band.

The Hierarchical Structure of the Church (#874-913)

Ministry exists in the Church so that Christ can provide for the nourishment and continued growth of the Church. In the Church there are ordained ministries and lay ministries. It needs to be stressed that ministers are not outside of or apart from the rest of the baptized; rather, they are chosen from among the baptized to serve all.

Ordained Ministers

Ordained ministers, authorized and empowered by Christ, must see themselves as servants of the Christian community. Ordained ministry has a collegial character. Every bishop of a local Church exercises his ministry within the college of bishops in communion with the bishop of Rome.

The *Catechism* moves almost too quickly from discussing ministry as service to speaking of it as "power." Supreme and full power over the Church is exercised in two ways: first, through the college of bishops united with the Pope as their head and, second, by the Pope alone as Bishop of Rome and successor of Saint Peter. As Vatican II says, the Roman Pontiff "by virtue of his office as vicar of Christ and shepherd of the whole Church" possesses "full, supreme and universal power, which he may always exercise freely, over the whole Church" (*Constitution on the Church*, #22).

Bishops in their local Churches have the power to teach, to sanctify and to govern by reason of their episcopal ordination. It is regrettable that, because the First Vatican Council concentrated on the powers of the pope and was forced to adjourn before discussing the role of the bishops, some people have come to think of bishops as delegates of the pope. Vatican II made clear that this is not the case. Bishops receive their power directly from God through their ordination. In fact, they too are called "vicars of Christ" in their local Churches (*Constitution on the Church*, #27). Bishops have concern not only for their local Churches, they also share with the pope a solicitude for all the Churches.

Lay Ministers

Readers whose memories go back a number of decades will perhaps recall that in the 1940s and 1950s lay involvement in the life of the Church was strongly encouraged. Pius XI called laypeople to Catholic Action, which he defined as "the participation of the laity in the apostolate of the hierarchy." Vatican II changed this understanding of lay ministry significantly: "The lay apostolate is a participation in the mission of the Church itself. Through their Baptism and Confirmation all are commissioned to that apostolate by the Lord himself" (*Constitution on the Church*, #33).

This clarification—that the Church's mission belongs to the laity as well as to the bishops—is most important at this time in the life of the Church, when the number of ordained ministers is drastically reduced. It can serve also as a reminder to us that our first thought about Church ought to be the realization that all of us, whether ordained or lay, have been constituted by Baptism as the People of God, an Easter people whose song is "Alleluia."

Growing in Knowledge

1) Why do we call the Church a sacrament?

2) What are some of the ways the Holy Spirit works to build up the Church?

3) Why is ecumenism important to Catholics?

4) How did Vatican II change our understanding of lay ministry?

Growing in Faith

1) What feelings does the word *Church* evoke in you?

2) Have you ever been angry at the Church? Why? How did you resolve it?

3) Have you ever been glad to be part of the Church? When and why?

4) How would you answer a friend who asked why you stay in the Church?

CHAPTER FOUR

Liturgy: Celebrating the Christian Mystery

> *It is [the] mystery of Christ that the Church proclaims and celebrates in her liturgy so that the faithful may live from it and bear witness to it in the world.*
> —Catechism of the Catholic Church, #1068

In the book of prayers used at liturgy, the Sacramentary, the text is in two colors: black and red. Only the text in black is spoken or sung in the liturgy. The text in red gives directions to the priest and other ministers. The Latin word for "red" is *ruber*; hence these texts were referred to as "rubrics." In my seminary days back in the 1940s, our course in liturgy was largely a course in rubrics. We were taught how to say Mass, how to administer the sacraments. Put simply, we studied the red text more diligently than the black.

The Action of Christ and His Church

One way of describing the changes that Vatican II effected in the liturgy is to say that it reversed our emphasis from the red text to the black. Like a successful business, we needed to be more in the black than in the red. For the text in black contains God's word to us and our response to God; that is where our principal concentration ought to be. Our chief concern, in other words, ought to be with *what we are doing*, not merely *how to do it.* This is not to say that the directives are unimportant. But they exist only to help us celebrate well the saving acts of God and our response to them.

Knowing the importance of the text in black opens our eyes to the words of Vatican II: "The liturgy is the summit toward which the activity of the Church is directed; at the same time it is the fountain from which all her power flows." Also, "[In the liturgy] full public worship is performed by the Mystical Body of Christ, that is by the Head and his members" (*Constitution on the Liturgy*, #10, 8; see *Catechism*, #1070). Liturgy, therefore, is the action of Christ and his Church, that shows the communion in Christ between God and God's people.

Liturgy and the Trinity (#1077-1109)

Liturgy is Trinitarian. It expresses the blessings that come from the Father from the beginning to the end of time. These blessings are especially manifested and communicated in Jesus Christ, who is the sacrament of God (that is, the effective sign that God is acting in the world in the midst of God's people). The Holy Spirit, who calls to our minds the divine blessings, is, in the words of the *Catechism*, "the Church's living memory" (#1099). The Spirit makes present in our midst the blessing of God and the action of the redeeming Christ.

The Work of God's People

But liturgy is not simply God's action that we passively attend or receive. Liturgy is not just the work of God; it is also the work of God's people. In fact, the word "liturgy" emphasizes this human aspect. It derives from the Greek word *laos*, which means "people" and *ergon* which means "work." All of God's people, therefore, are called, not just to *be* at liturgy, but actively to "work" at it.

While the priest, by virtue of Holy Orders, *presides* at the liturgy, the whole Body of Christ *celebrates* it. "The celebrating assembly is the community of the baptized who...'are consecrated to be a spiritual house and a holy priesthood, that...they may offer spiritual sacrifices.' This 'common priesthood' is that of Christ the sole priest, in which all his members participate" (*Catechism*, #1141, quoting the *Constitution on the Church*, #10). Citing the *Constitution on the Liturgy* (#14), the *Catechism* adds that it then follows that the Church "earnestly desires that all the faithful should be led to that full, conscious, and active participation in liturgical celebrations which is demanded by the very nature of liturgy, and to which the Christian people, 'a chosen race, a royal priesthood, a holy nation, a redeemed people' [see 1 Peter 2:9], have a right and an obligation by reason of their Baptism."

Different Ministries (#1142)

While all are called to celebrate liturgy, we do not all have the same function. The priest, empowered by the sacrament of Holy Orders, presides over the liturgy and acts in the person of Christ in the service of all the members of the Church. Other particular ministries, not involving Holy Orders, are exercises of the priesthood of the faithful: "Servers, readers, commentators, and members of the choir also exercise a genuine liturgical function" (*Constitution on the Liturgy*, #29). To this list we may also add ministers of the Eucharist and ministers of hospitality.

Besides these "special ministries," there is the celebratory participation of all the faithful of Christ. For all who are present take part in the liturgy by means of acclamations, responses, psalms, antiphons and songs and, especially, by participating in the eucharistic meal at the table of the Lord. A contemplative silence observed at appropriate times in the liturgy (for example, after the call to pray, after the readings, after the homily, at the time of Communion) is also a fruitful way of participating in liturgy.

For a person who wishes to live the Christian life, participation in liturgy is not an option but a must. To be present at Sunday liturgy without making any desire or effort to participate leaves much of the Sunday obligation unfulfilled.

The Language of Liturgy: Signs and Symbols (#1145-1152)

The language of the liturgy is the language of sign and symbol. We tell the story of our faith over and over again and, because words can never adequately tell that story, we make use of symbols. This is true, as the *Catechism* points out, of all the great religions of the world. Signs and symbols are the common language of those who wish to talk about the Transcendent (#1149).

Christian faith makes use of signs and symbols drawn from the world of creation: water, fire, oil. Some symbols come from human life: washing, anointing, touching, breaking and sharing bread. Symbols are also derived from God's saving actions: the passage over the Red Sea, manna in the desert. Incorporated into Christian rituals, such symbols help us to understand the world of faith and the power of the Holy Spirit.

The symbols become bearers of God's saving action in Christ. For example, we use water in Baptism. Water is an ambiguous symbol: It means destruction, as in the waters of a flood. It is also a symbol of cleansing and, falling upon the earth and making it fruitful, a symbol of life. All these meanings are picked up in our baptismal rites, where the baptized enter into the death and resurrection of Christ. The Spirit of God makes the waters fruitful. Sin is destroyed; new life is received. The newly baptized enter into the communion of the Body of Christ.

We use oil as a symbol of healing. And in our most important liturgical celebration, the Eucharist, we use simple, ordinary food, bread and wine. The action of the Holy Spirit confers on them a new and transcendent meaning.

The liturgy also uses symbolic language—poetry, music. The harmony of song and music, words and actions embodies the beauty and power of our Christian heritage and expresses in its diversity the cultural richness of the people of God (*Catechism*, #1158).

Celebrating and Deepening Faith

The way we celebrate liturgy not only expresses faith but also deepens it. A superb clarification of this important insight appears in a statement made in 1968 by the American Bishops' Committee on the Liturgy. They are speaking specifically about the Eucharist, but what they say can be applied to all liturgical celebrations. In a document called *Music in Catholic Worship*, they tell us:

> We are Christians because through the Christian community we have met Jesus Christ, heard his word in invitation, and responded to him in faith. We gather

> at Mass that we may hear and express our faith again in this assembly and, by expressing it, renew and deepen it.
>
> We do not come to meet Christ as if he were absent from the rest of our lives. We come together to deepen our awareness of, and commitment to, the action of his Spirit in the whole of our lives at every moment. We come together to acknowledge the love of God poured out among us in the work of the Spirit, to stand in awe and praise.

The bishops' statement uses the spousal relationship as a powerful image of what they are saying about liturgy:

> People in love make signs of love, not only to express their love but also to deepen it. Love never expressed dies. Christians' love for Christ and for one another must be expressed in the signs and symbols of celebration or they will die.

That statement puts liturgy in touch with people's real life. It poses a problem people may sometimes encounter in worship and suggests a solution: We may not feel like celebrating on this or that Sunday, even though we are called by the Church's law to do so. Our faith does not always permeate our feelings. But this is the function of signs in the Church: to give bodily expression to faith, to transform our fragile awareness of Christ's presence in the dark of our daily isolation into a joyful, integral experience of his liberating action in the solidarity of the celebrating community.

Finally, the Bishops' statement draws a conclusion which is well worth the reflection of parish liturgy committees and liturgy planners: It is clear that the manner in which the Church celebrates the liturgy has an effect on people. "Good celebrations foster and nourish faith. Poor celebrations may weaken and destroy faith."

What is very evident from this statement is the fact that liturgy cannot be a hothouse celebration separate from the real life of people living in the world. It highlights also the importance of the planning of liturgical celebrations properly. Good liturgies do not just happen.

The bishops' text goes on to stress, as does the *Catechism*, the importance of the Lord's Day. The *Catechism* puts it clearly:

> The day of Christ's Resurrection is both the first day of the week, the memorial of the first day of creation, and the "eighth day," on which Christ after his "rest" on the great sabbath inaugurates the "day that the Lord has made," the "day that knows no evening." The Lord's Supper is its center, for there the whole community of the faithful encounters the risen Lord who invites them to his banquet" (#1166).

Saint Jerome, remembering that the Romans called Sunday the day of the sun god, picks up this image and says strikingly: "Today is revealed the sun of justice with healing in his rays."

The Liturgical Year (#1168-1171)

We think of the liturgical year as beginning with Advent, but its real beginning, in the sense of the point from which it draws all its meaning, is the Easter Triduum. The Triduum spreads its brilliance through the whole of the Church's year. This was clearly evident in the earliest days of the Church, when the mystery of Jesus' Resurrection was the only mystery celebrated. Each Sunday was a weekly Easter; very early a special Sunday, coinciding with the Jewish Passover season, became the annual celebration of Christ's Paschal Mystery. Soon the celebration was spread over two days, then later over three—the three days that came to be called the "Easter Triduum." (Following our Jewish ancestors' method of marking time, the day begins at sundown. Thus the Triduum begins Holy Thursday evening and ends Easter evening.)

Eventually the Triduum was surrounded by Lent on one side (as a time of preparation for the catechumens and later a time of penance for those who were guilty of certain grave and public sins) and on the other side by the Easter Season, a time for seeking deeper insight into the mysteries experienced in the Triduum. The Easter season culminated in the feasts of the Ascension and Pentecost.

Some time in the fourth century the feast of Christmas was celebrated in Rome on December 25 (even earlier the birth-feast was celebrated on Epiphany in the East). There are traces of a period of preparation for Christmas (Advent) as early as the fifth century. But even the feasts centering about the mystery of the Incarnation derive their light and significance from the mystery of Easter. As the Catechism puts it: "In the liturgical year the various aspects of the one Paschal mystery unfold. This is also the case with the cycle of feasts surrounding the mystery of the incarnation (Annunciation, Christmas, Epiphany). They commemorate the beginning of our salvation and communicate to us the first fruits of the Paschal mystery" (#1171).

Thus, in a most fundamental sense, there is only one liturgical theme: the Paschal Mystery of the death and resurrection of the Lord.

The Liturgy of the Hours (#1174-1178)

From early Christian times, it has been the practice of the Church to fill the day and night with the praise of God. This is achieved through the Liturgy of the Hours (or, as we used to call it, the Divine Office). The Liturgy of the Hours is made up of (1) the Office of Readings, (2) Morning Prayer (Lauds), (3) Daytime prayer (midmorning, midday or midafternoon), (4) Evening Prayer (Vespers) and (5) Night Prayer (Compline).

While some people—priests and religious—are officially charged with praying the Liturgy of the Hours, it is really intended to be the prayer of the whole Church, the prayer that Christ and his Body address to God. Hence all are encouraged to participate in it. Special importance is given to Morning Prayer and Evening Prayer, which the *Constitution on the Liturgy* describes as "the two hinges on which the daily Office turns" (#89).

Many parishes are making an effort to revive the celebration of Sunday Vespers, once a normal part of the observance of the Lord's Day. As Sunday becomes more and more commercialized, it is important that we restore to Sunday the sacred character it has had in the Church from apostolic times onward. In an unpublished work called *The Inner Experience*, Thomas Merton writes inspiringly about Sunday: "Sunday is a day of contemplation, because it is sacred to the mystery of the Resurrection."

Sunday is the Lord's Day "not in the sense that on one day out of the week, one must stop and think of God, but because it breaks into the ceaseless 'secular' round of time with a burst of light out of a sacred eternity."

We stop working and rushing about on Sunday not only in order to rest up and start over again on Monday, but in order to collect our wits and savor the peace given us by Christ that surpasses understanding. Sunday then becomes a reminder to us of the peace that should filter through the whole week when our work is properly oriented.

"Everyone who celebrates the day spiritually and accepts it at its face value opens his or her heart to the light of Christ, the light of the resurrection. In so doing a person grows in love, in faith, and is able to 'see' a little more of the mystery of Christ."

And it is that mystery which, in the words of the *Catechism*, "the Church proclaims and celebrates in her liturgy so that the faithful may live from it and bear witness to it in the world" (#1068).

Growing in Knowledge

1) How is liturgy the "work" of the Church?

2) Why is the Easter Triduum the "real beginning" of the Church year?

3) Why is Sunday important in Christian life?

4) What is the Liturgy of the Hours?

GROWING IN FAITH

1) Are you a liturgical minister? If so, what drew you to that particular ministry?

2) What signs and symbols have you used to express experiences difficult to put into words?

3) What liturgies have truly nourished and deepened your faith?

4) How is Sunday different from the rest of the week in your home?

CHAPTER FIVE

The Sacraments of Christian Initiation

> *From the time of the apostles, becoming a Christian has been accomplished by a journey and initiation in several stages.*—Catechism of the Catholic Church, #1229

When I was first ordained a priest a half-century ago, the standard fare used for instructing converts was the well-known classic, *Father Smith Instructs Jackson*. It was the *Baltimore Catechism* in drama form. The drama consisted of a dialogue between Mr. Jackson, a would-be "convert," who comes to the Catholic rectory each week for a lesson, and his instructor, Father Smith, the parish priest. Both are remarkable people. On each visit Mr. Jackson brings a lot of perceptive questions. But he never stumps Father Smith! As the plot unfolds, one cannot help but admire Father Smith's remarkable astuteness. He never fails to come up with a splendid answer. Not once does Mr. Jackson leave the rectory with an unanswered question.

After reading this book under the tutelage of a priest, the would-be convert was ready for Baptism. The parish priest would use the Rite of Baptism designed for infants, slightly adapting it for an adult. The Baptism would be a private affair. Present with the new convert would be the sponsor and perhaps a few friends. No community involvement was necessary: Baptism was seen as a way for achieving personal salvation. Then on Sunday the new Catholic would approach the Communion rail for the first time, to the surprise (but probably not much to the concern), of people who had known him or her simply as a non-Catholic.

Christian Initiation (#1229-1245)

Today a book for a person wishing to become a Catholic would have to bear a very different title. It might be: *Welcome Jackson!* with the subtitle, *Father Smith and the Community of Saint Paul's Parish Initiates Jackson*. Actually, such a book already exists, though it carries quite a different title. Called *The Rite of Christian Initiation of Adults*, it calls for much more than a *tête à tête* between Father Smith and Jackson. It has revolutionized the steps whereby a person is received into the Church.

The whole community is involved in the process of the Jacksons' journey toward full initiation into the Church. That journey goes through three basic stages. There is, first of all, a *precatechumenate* stage, during which the inquirers search for the will of God and hear the gospel message proclaimed. Once they have reached the point of accepting the gospel and wish to be received into the Church, they enter the Order of Catechumens, usually with a group of others who are at the same point of the journey.

Catechumenate

The catechumenate, which may last for several years, involves instruction (catechesis) as well as liturgical rites, including celebrations of the word of God, exorcisms, blessings and anointing with the oil of the catechumens. These events take place in the midst of the community and end with the ceremony of election.

Election and Initiation

The third and final stage, which takes place during Lent, prepares the elect for the actual reception of the sacraments of initiation—Baptism, Confirmation and First Eucharist—at the Easter Vigil Service. The newly baptized are embraced with love and joy by the community of Easter people, whose song is "alleluia."

Post-Baptismal Catechesis

To strengthen those just baptized (the neophytes), a period of post-baptismal catechesis follows during the Easter season. This form of catechesis has a very long history in the Church; there are many examples of it in homilies by the early Fathers of the Church. Called *mystagogia*, which means a deeper explanation of the mysteries into which the newly baptized have been initiated, it emphasizes the great care that must be taken to assure the full and joyful insertion of the new members into the life of the community.

This did not happen to me or to most of the Catholics I know. We were all baptized as infants. Confirmation was postponed for several years and usually took place after First Communion. This is true and it continues to be the case with those who are baptized as infants. Yet "usual" does not necessarily mean "ideal." The new *Rite of Christian Initiation of Adults* makes it clear that the full initiation which this Rite prescribes is the standard for initiation into the Church.

Strangely enough, till this new Rite came into being, there was no initiation rite for adults (at least not one that was commonly used). Hence, when adults were received into the Church, the rite used was that for the Baptism of children, adapted to the person's adult status. Now the mind of the Church is that it should be the other way round. The rite for adults is the established norm. When children are baptized, the rite used telescopes the stages of initiation into a single, much abridged ceremony.

This means that the catechesis presented to adults before Baptism must be given to children baptized as infants *after* their Baptism, when they are old enough to appreciate it. It is precisely to aid catechists in carrying out the responsibility of catechizing baptized children that the *Catechism of the Catholic Church* (as well as any local adaptations of it) has come into being.

But use of the *Catechism* is not restricted to children. It also has a place in the prebaptismal catechesis of adults. Furthermore, many adults baptized in infancy are very much in need of further catechesis. The *Catechism* is intended, therefore, to serve a wide need in the Church.

The Three Sacraments of Initiation

The Rite of Christian Initiation of Adults speaks not just of one sacrament of initiation, but of three: Baptism, Confirmation and Eucharist. Initiation into the Church community is not completed till all three sacraments have been celebrated. The clear linkage of these sacraments is expressed in the Eastern Rites of the Church where, even in the case of infants, Baptism is followed immediately by Confirmation and First Eucharist. In the Roman Rite the infant Baptism is followed by years of catechesis before the initiation is completed by Confirmation and Eucharist.

Among Catholics of the Roman Rite there is much unresolved discussion about Confirmation: is it a part of initiation or a rite of passage into adulthood? The *Catechism of the Catholic Church*, as well as other Church documents, seems to be very clear that it belongs to initiation and, moreover, that the traditional order of Baptism, Confirmation and Eucharist should be restored. How this is to be worked out pastorally is still very much under discussion.

Baptism (#1213-1284)

Baptism is an immersion or submersion into water by which those who profess their faith in Christ are born again by the power of the Holy Spirit into new life. They become members of Christ, are incorporated into his Church and made sharers in his mission.

The Symbolism of Water. In the natural order, water can be a sign of life and fruitfulness; for example, the rain that falls to the ground to water the crops and make them grow. It can also be a sign of destructiveness: torrential and long-lasting rains can produce floods and destroy property, crops and even people.

Biblical Symbolism. The waters of the flood in Noah's time were a source of life for a few and destruction for many. The waters of the Red Sea symbolized the liberation of Israel from the slavery of Egypt and entrance into new life—and also destruction for the armies of Egypt. The crossing of the Jordan River by the Israelites signaled the end to their time of homeless wandering and their entrance into the land God had promised to their ancestors.

Jesus' Baptism. Jesus' baptism by John in the Jordan River was a sign of his own self-emptying. It was accompanied by the descent of God's Spirit upon him and the voice of the Father proclaiming him the Beloved on whom God's favor rested. During his ministry, Jesus speaks of a baptism he is to undergo: "I have a baptism with which to be baptized, and what stress I am under until it is completed!" (Luke 12:50). The reference is to his Passion, whereby he is plunged into death and then raised from the dead to new life. His baptism—the Paschal Mystery—was his symbolic passage through the Red Sea and through the waters of the Jordan, a passover from mortal existence to new and immortal life.

The Meaning of Christian Baptism

1) *Baptism is a bath* that washes away our sins and incorporates us into the Paschal Mystery of the Lord Jesus. Submerged into the waters of Baptism, we die and are buried with Christ; brought up out of the waters, we rise with Christ into new life. As Paul writes: "Do you not know that all of us who have been baptized into Christ Jesus were baptized into his death? Therefore we have been buried with him by baptism into death, so that, just as Christ was raised from the dead by the glory of the Father, so we too might walk in newness of life" (Romans 6:3-4). The baptismal font is a tomb into which the catechumens descend and die to the old self; it becomes the womb out of which they rise, born into new life. During the Easter Vigil blessing of the font, the Paschal candle, in a deeply symbolic action, is plunged three times into the water with a prayer that the Holy Spirit may make these waters fruitful.

2) In Baptism *we receive the Holy Spirit* whom the risen Jesus sent upon his Church. On the day of Pentecost Peter preaches to the crowds, inviting them to repent and be baptized. Then their sins will be forgiven and they will receive the gift of the Holy Spirit (see Acts 2:38). The Holy Spirit is the Spirit of truth who continually recalls what Jesus taught and leads us

into the truth. As the *Catechism* expresses it so beautifully: "The Holy Spirit is the Church's living memory" (#1099).

3) Plunging us into the Paschal Mystery of Christ and bringing the Holy Spirit into our lives, Baptism *incorporates us into the Church*, the community of God's people. We become members of Christ, united with him and in him with one another. In the image used by Saint Paul, we are the Body of Christ.

4) Baptism is *empowerment*. By reason of our Baptism we share in the mission of Christ and of the Church. (See Chapter Three for further discussion of the baptismal call to mission.)

5) Baptism is the *fundamental source of Christian dignity*. There is no greater Christian dignity than to be a baptized person: This was a fundamental emphasis in the documents of the Second Vatican Council, particularly the document on the Church. It was spelled out quite concretely at a liturgy celebrated by the Council Fathers in the autumn of 1963. The liturgy was in remembrance of Pope John XXIII, who had died on June 3 of that year. In the course of his tribute to Pope John, Cardinal Suenens, the homilist, said: "The greatest day in the life of Pope John was not the day he became pope or the day he was ordained a bishop; neither was it the day he was ordained a priest. The greatest day in the life of Pope John was the day on which he was baptized into Christ."

The cardinal's words were clearly not intended to deny that those who exercise hierarchical authority in the Church are empowered by God to do so. But the exercise of different roles in the Church is in no way a denial of the equal dignity that identifies everyone baptized into Christ. Those who exercise authority in the Church are baptized persons chosen from among the baptized to minister to all the baptized.

6) Baptism is the *sacramental bond of Christian unity*. It offers the foundation for ecumenical dialogue. All who believe in Christ and have been validly baptized are in communion with one another, although that communion remains imperfect as long as the divisions among Christians persist. As the *Catechism*, quoting the Vatican II document on ecumenism, puts it: "Justified by faith in Baptism, [they] are incorporated into Christ; they therefore have a right to be called Christians,

and with good reason are accepted as brothers [and sisters] in the Lord by the children of the Catholic Church" (#1271).

7) Baptism *imparts an indelible spiritual mark upon the soul*, a seal of the Spirit, which consecrates the baptized for Christian worship in the common priesthood of all the faithful. As the First Letter of Peter says: "...[Y]ou are a chosen race, *a royal priesthood*, a holy nation, God's own people, in order that you may proclaim the mighty acts of him who called you out of darkness into his marvelous light" (1 Peter 2:9, emphasis added).

The Necessity of Baptism

Jesus affirmed the necessity of Baptism. To Nicodemus, his night visitor, Jesus said: "Very truly, I tell you, no one can enter the kingdom of God without being born of water and Spirit" (John 3:5b). Mark narrates that, as Jesus was about to ascend to the Father, he commanded his disciples to proclaim the gospel and to baptize: "The one who believes and is baptized will be saved" (Mark 16:16a). Thus, the Church knows no other means of assuring salvation but Baptism.

The *Catechism* makes clear, however, that the necessity of Baptism is not absolute. God can save in whatever way God chooses. "*God has bound salvation to the sacrament of Baptism, but he himself is not bound by his sacraments*" (#1257). Moreover, the Church explicitly teaches certain exceptions. People martyred for the faith, catechumens who die before being baptized, people who, without knowing the Church but moved by God's grace, seek God sincerely and strive to do God's will: These can be saved even though they have not been baptized (#1281).

The Demise of Limbo

One of the painful pastoral problems that had to be dealt with in the past was the fate of unbaptized children. Bereaved parents whose children died without Baptism had laid upon them the additional grief of thinking that their children would never see God face-to-face. For all eternity they would be consigned to the Limbo of the children.

Mercifully, the *Catechism* has "abolished" Limbo. It points out that the Church can only entrust children who have died without Baptism to God's mercy, as it does in the funeral rites for them. Indeed, the great mercy of God, who desires that all people should be saved, and Jesus' tenderness towards children, which caused him to say: "Let the little children come to me; do not stop them" (Mark 10:14), allows us to hope that there is a way of salvation for children who have died without Baptism (see #1261).

Confirmation (#1285-1321)

As a sacrament of initiation, Confirmation is intimately linked with Baptism and Eucharist. Christians are reborn in Baptism, strengthened by Confirmation and sustained by the food of the Eucharist. Confirmation *confirms* the Baptism: It is a fuller outpouring of the Spirit, incorporating us more completely into Christ and strengthening us in our call to participate in the mission of the Church and in the building of the Kingdom.

The ordinary minister of the sacrament is the bishop, but he may for pastoral reasons delegate this ministry to priests. In the Latin rite, the bishop prays over the candidates and then confers the sacrament through anointing with chrism (oil blessed by the bishop on or near Holy Thursday for use in the whole diocese). This is done with a laying on of the hands and with the words: "Be sealed with the gift of the Holy Spirit."

In the earliest days of the Church, when the local Church was a single community presided over by the bishop, a person would go before the bishop immediately after Baptism to receive the Confirmation or chrismation. Then the baptized would participate in the Eucharist.

When local Churches became so large that the bishop could not be present at every Baptism and infant Baptism became common, a choice had to be made between two alternatives. Should the three sacraments of initiation be kept together and therefore be conferred by the parish priest when the bishop could not be present? Or was the conferring of Confirmation by the bishop so important that Confirmation should be delayed until the bishop could come?

The Eastern Rites chose the first alternative and gave priority to the unity of the sacraments of initiation. Hence, in the absence of the bishop, Confirmation is conferred by the priest who baptizes a baby. The Roman Rite chose the second alternative, emphasizing the importance of the bishop's presence, and separated Confirmation from Baptism, postponing it until the bishop was available. To show the link with Confirmation, the priest at the time of Baptism anoints the candidate with chrism.

In the Roman Rite Confirmation is administered after the age of reason has been reached. But there is considerable disagreement as to the precise age for Confirmation. Practice differs widely from place to place.

The Holy Eucharist

The Holy Eucharist completes Christian initiation. Those who have been given the dignity of Christ's royal priesthood by Baptism and strengthened in their Christian commitment by Confirmation participate with the whole Christian community in the Eucharist.

Since the Eucharist is "the source and summit of the Christian life" (#1324), a detailed discussion of the Eucharist will be the topic of the next chapter.

GROWING IN KNOWLEDGE

1) What are the three stages of preparation for initiation?

2) Why is it fitting that Baptism be a parish celebration rather than a private or family celebration?

3) Why is the theory of limbo no longer being taught?

4) What is the mystagogia?

Growing in Faith

1) If you were baptized as an infant, how have you lived the promises made for you by your parents and godparents?

2) How has the new rite for the initiation of adults touched your life or the life of your parish?

3) If you are a godparent, how have you helped your godchild live the baptismal promises?

4) How can water be a reminder of Baptism in your daily life?

CHAPTER SIX

The Eucharist: 'What Time Is Church?'

> *The Eucharist commits us to the poor. To receive in truth the Body and Blood of Christ given up for us, we must recognize Christ in the poorest, his [brothers and sisters].*—Catechism of the Catholic Church, #1397

Some years ago, when I was an associate at Sacred Heart Cathedral in Rochester, New York, I used to help out once a week at nearby St. Anthony's. One day a young boy asked me: "Father, what time is Church next Sunday?" I chided him for not asking, "What time is Mass?" As I reflect now on his question, it embodies—though I doubt if he realized it—a fine perspective on both Church and Eucharist.

"What time is Church?" The Church exists at all times, but the moment of Eucharist is a special time in the Church's life. It is the time when the people of God, scattered throughout the week, gather together at God's call to celebrate over and over again the memorial of the death and resurrection of the Lord. The time when the Eucharist is celebrated is an especially appropriate answer to the question, "What time is Church?"

The Holy Eucharist completes the initiation of Christians. Participation in the Eucharist is the exercise of the royal priesthood conferred on the People of God by the other sacraments of initiation: Baptism and Confirmation.

A Rich Sacrament (#1322-1332)

The inexhaustible richness of this sacrament cannot be

conveyed in a single term. We make use of many names, therefore, to describe it. Yet no single name or series of names can adequately explain this wondrous reality. It remains always the "mystery of Faith." The following are some of the names we use to speak about that mystery. Each offers a slightly different way of understanding what we can never fully understand.

Names for the Sacrament

Eucharist. We call it the Eucharist because it is an act of thanksgiving and praise for God's wonderful works on our behalf: creation, redemption and sanctification. The Greek word *eucharistein* means "to give thanks."

The Lord's Supper recalls the meal Jesus shared with his disciples on the eve of his Passion, the meal at which he washed their feet and gave them his Body and Blood.

The Breaking of Bread was probably the earliest name used to designate the Eucharist. The Acts of Apostles describes the early Christian community at Jerusalem as devoting themselves "to the apostles' teaching and fellowship, to the breaking of bread and the prayers" (Acts 2:42). Luke tells us that the two disciples at Emmaus recognized the risen Jesus "in the breaking of bread" (see Luke 24:13-35). Jesus' gesture at the Last Supper and at other meals recalls the Jewish custom of breaking bread to share with those at table. The breaking of the one loaf to share with the many expresses the communion Jesus wills to enter into with his followers.

The Eucharistic Assembly. The very gathering of the community is an expression of the Church at worship. It is the time when the community becomes especially alive and aware of its oneness in the Lord.

Memorial (Anamnesis). We remember the Lord's Passion and Resurrection, as he commanded us: "Do this in memory of me." In the Scriptures a memorial is both a recollection of what God has done in the past and at the same time a proclamation of what God is doing now. In the liturgical celebration past events and their power to save become present realities in the life of the community. In the Eucharist the Lord's passover from death to life is made present and effective in the life of the worshiping community.

The Holy Sacrifice. Since it is a memorial of Christ's passover, his body given up for us, his blood shed for us, the Eucharist is also a sacrifice. It represents (makes present) the one sacrifice of the cross. Joined to Jesus' sacrifice is also the sacrifice of the Church, as God's people unite their own lives, prayers, praise, daily work to the sacrifice of Christ. Just as Christ intercedes for us, so the Church intercedes for its members and for the whole world. In early Christian art the Church is sometimes represented as a woman with arms extended wide in prayer. Like Christ, who stretched out his arms on the cross, the Church, through him, with him and in him, offers herself and intercedes for all peoples (#1362-1368).

The Most Blessed Sacrament. The sacrament is most blessed because the Eucharist is the peak moment of the Church's liturgical life. All the other sacraments are directed toward it and find their culmination in it. This term is also used to describe the Eucharistic elements reserved in the tabernacle.

Communion. In this sacrament we are united to Christ. By sharing his Body and Blood, we become one Body with him. "Communion with the flesh of the risen Christ...preserves, increases, and renews the life of grace received at Baptism" (#1392). Communion also builds the Church. It makes us one Body with Christ. A very ancient saying has it: *Eucharistia facit ecclesiam* ("The Eucharist makes the Church"). We are called to communion especially with the least of Christ's brothers and sisters: the poor and other victims of oppression and injustice.

Mass. This term is used in the Latin Church, because the liturgy concludes with a sending forth (*missio*) of the faithful to live and proclaim the gospel message.

The Pledge of Future Glory. While this is not a name we ordinarily use to describe the Eucharist, it does speak of the ultimate direction in which the Eucharist points us. As we celebrate the Eucharist, "we wait in joyful hope for the coming of our Savior Jesus Christ." The Eucharist not only makes the past present (*anamnesis*), it also projects us into the ultimate future, as we long for the final completion of God's kingdom (#1402-1404).

Historical Background (#1333-1344)

The Eucharist was prefigured in the Old Testament in a number of events; for example, the bread and wine offered by that mysterious king-priest of Salem, Melchizedek (see Genesis 14:18-20); the unleavened bread eaten by the people of Israel each year at Passover, when they recalled their hasty escape from Egyptian slavery (see Exodus 12:14-20); the manna in the desert whereby God fed the people who had been saved from slavery (see Exodus 16:1-15); the "cup of blessing" taken at the close of the Passover meal.

In the New Testament the Eucharist is foreshadowed in the feeding of the multitude. Feeding the people who had been listening to Jesus and afterwards were hungry but without food is of special importance to the Gospel writers. It is the only event before the passion narratives that is described in all four of the Gospels (see Matthew 14:13-21; Mark 6:32-44; Luke 9:10-17; John 6:1-13). In each case Jesus uses gestures that are obviously eucharistic: He has the bread brought to him; he blesses it, breaks it and distributes it to feed the many.

The many meals that Jesus took during his ministry with sinners and the outcasts of society also prefigure the Eucharist as a sacrament that embodies the forgiving and reconciling love of God and reminds us of our responsibility to show concern for the needs of the poor (#1397).

The Last Supper

Jesus instituted the Eucharist on the night before he died. Knowing that he was about to return to the Father, he loved his own to the end. He shared a meal with them. He washed their feet as a symbolic expression of the new commandment of love he gave to them: "I give you a new commandment, that you love one another. Just as I have loved you, you also should love one another" (John 13:34). At the Last Supper Jesus gave his followers the Eucharist as a memorial of his death and resurrection and commanded his disciples to do what he had done in memory of him until the end of time.

It is worth noting that the three Synoptic Gospels (Matthew, Mark and Luke) and Saint Paul describe the words of institution. John's Gospel, on the other hand, does not include those words in its narrative of the Supper, but instead narrates the foot-washing ceremony. The others tell us what Jesus *said* at the supper; the fourth Gospel tells us what Jesus *did*.

The action explains the words. What Jesus did for his disciples tells us that the Eucharist is a sign of the loving service we owe to one another. The *Catechism* quotes a moving passage from a sermon of Saint Augustine, in which he compares the Body of Christ in the Eucharist to the Body of Christ which is the Church:

> If you are the body and members of Christ, then it is your sacrament that is placed on the table of the Lord; it is your sacrament that you receive. To that which you are you respond "Amen" ("yes, it is true!") and by responding to it you assent to it. For you hear the words, "the Body of Christ" and respond "Amen." Be then a member of the Body of Christ that your *Amen* may be true. (#1396)

Eucharist in the Early Church

From the very beginning, the Church has been faithful to the Lord's command: "Do this in memory of me." Especially on Sunday, the "first day of the week," the day of Jesus' Resurrection, Christians met "to break bread." Saint Justin Martyr, writing in the middle of the second century, describes the basic structure of the Eucharist. It included the gathering of the assembly, the reading of the "memoirs of the apostles and the writings of the prophets," the bringing up of bread and wine, a Eucharistic Prayer (a prayer of thanksgiving and praise) said by the one who presides, the "Amen" of all present and the distribution of the bread and the cup to them. The bread and cup are then taken by the deacons to those who are not present (#1345).

Reservation of the Eucharist

For some centuries, the only reason for reserving the Eucharist was to provide Communion for the sick. In the Middle Ages, a development of eucharistic piety led to the veneration of the reserved species. Liturgical directives today direct that the tabernacle should be placed in a special chapel. If that is not possible, it should be located in the church in a place of honor that is suitably adorned and where people may come for personal prayer and devotion.

The Liturgical Celebration of the Eucharist (#1345-1355)

Though the way of celebrating the Eucharist has varied considerably through history, the basic structure has remained the same: There are two main parts which form one act of worship: the Liturgy of the Word of God and the Liturgy of the Eucharist. Introductory rites precede the Liturgy of the Word and concluding rites follow the Liturgy of the Eucharist.

Liturgy of the Word

The *Introductory Rites.* Through these rites, the assembled people of God become conscious of themselves as a community, ready to hear God's Word, to celebrate the sacrificial self-giving of Jesus and to share a meal which expresses and deepens their oneness with Christ and in him with one another. They become aware that, even as they gather, *Christ is already present among them.* For he said that where two or three are gathered together in his name, he is there in the midst of them (see #1373; Matthew 18:20).

Christ is the head who presides over every Eucharist. He is represented by the presiding bishop or priest. All God's people have active parts to play in the celebration: readers, gift-bearers, eucharistic ministers and the whole people with their songs and acclamations.

The *Readings.* The Liturgy of the Word includes readings from the Old Testament and the New. (The final reading is always from the Gospels.) *Christ becomes present to us through the Word of Scripture* proclaimed in the assembly (see #1373).

To proclaim means more than to read. Reading communicates information or instruction. Proclamation does this and more: It challenges, it confronts, it makes demands. It also soothes and comforts, heartens and brings cheer. All this suggests the importance of thorough training of lectors to help them understand the importance of their ministry and the most effective ways of carrying it out. The high point of the liturgy of the Word is the *Gospel*, in which Christ continues to speak to his people, calling them to faith and conversion.

The *homily*, which Vatican II restored to its place as an integral part of the liturgy, is neither exegesis of Scripture (critical analysis of the text) nor moral exhortation. Rather it is a "breaking open" of the Word. Its purpose is to help the assembled community see how God is continuing to speak and act among God's people in the changing circumstances of the present.

The *General Intercessions*, prayers for all peoples and their needs, follow the homily.

The Liturgy of the Eucharist

The *preparation of the altar and the gifts.* The book of prayers (the Sacramentary) and the bread and wine are brought to the altar. The Creator's gifts are placed in the hands of Christ who brings to perfection all human attempts to offer sacrifice.

The *Eucharistic Prayer.* Center and summit of the Eucharistic celebration, the Eucharistic Prayer is a statement of praise and thanksgiving for God's works of salvation, as well as the action which *makes* the Eucharist, rendering present both the Lord's Body and Blood and his great redeeming actions. In poetic and biblical language the presiding priest addresses God; he speaks to and on behalf of the whole assembly. The assembly professes its faith and gives its assent by joining in the initial dialogue and the acclamations. All join themselves and their own self-giving to the total self-giving of Christ.

The Eucharistic Prayer has several closely connected elements:

The *Preface.* The word means "proclamation," not "introduction." In the Preface the Church gives praise and thanks to the Father through Christ in the Spirit for God's works of creation, redemption and sanctification.

The *Epiclesis* (invocation of the Holy Spirit). The Father is asked to send the Holy Spirit for the transformation of both the gifts and the assembled community. Thus, in the Second Eucharistic Prayer, we ask: "Let your Spirit come upon *these gifts* to make them holy, so that they may become for us the body and blood of our Lord Jesus Christ." And we later pray: "May *all of us* who share in the body and blood of Christ be brought together in unity by the Holy Spirit" (Eucharistic Prayer II, emphasis added).

The *Institution Narrative.* The power of the words of Christ and the action of the Holy Spirit make sacramentally present, under the species of bread and wine, the Body and Blood of Christ. *This is the real presence of Christ par excellence.*

The *Anamnesis* (Memorial). In obedience to Christ's command, the Church remembers (celebrates the memorial of) the Lord's passion and resurrection and looks forward to his coming in glory.

The *Offering.* The Church presents to God the gift of Jesus Christ, who reconciles us with God. It is an offering that is sacrificial, for we offer the body broken for us and the blood shed for us. The offering of the faithful—their prayers, sufferings, works—are joined to Christ's offering. Thus the Eucharist becomes our offering too.

The *Intercessions*, which make clear that every Eucharist is celebrated in communion with the entire Church and the whole Communion of Saints. In the Roman Canon (Eucharistic Prayer I), intercessions before and after the Institution Narrative are linked with the remembrance of the saints. In the newer Eucharistic Prayers, the intercessions are joined to the *epiclesis* said over the people. They include a general request to share in the blessings of the Eucharist and specific remembrances for the Church, its ministers and members, the dead.

In remembering the Blessed Virgin, the apostles, martyrs and all the saints, as well as the dead, the living who offer the Eucharist are already anticipating the heavenly banquet, which the Eucharist prefigures. Note how all of God's creation is brought together in the Eucharistic Prayer—from the angels (in the Holy, Holy) to the good things of the earth to the whole Communion of Saints.

The *final Doxology.* The Eucharistic Prayer comes to a conclusion with a marvelous (one wants to say "smashing!")

summing up of the praise/thanks theme which threads its way through the entire prayer. This conclusion is called the "lesser doxology" (expression of praise) to distinguish it from the greater doxology, the Glory to God in the Highest. The bread and cup are raised on high in a gesture of offering, as the doxology is said or sung by the one presiding at the Eucharist. It ends with the resounding "Amen!" of the worshiping community.

The *acclamations.* It should be noted that the three acclamations of the people—at the beginning (the Holy, Holy), in the middle (the Memorial Acclamation) and at the end (the Great Amen)—make clear that, while proclaimed by the priest, the Eucharistic Prayer is indeed the prayer of the entire assembly or, better still, the prayer of Christ and his people.

Communion. Communion expresses both reconciliation and the oneness that follows from it. In the Lord's Prayer we pray for the perfect establishment of God's reign and ask for forgiveness in terms of the forgiveness we offer to others. We pray for peace, the peace that comes from forgiveness given and received.

The *Sign of Peace* is more than the exchange of a jolly greeting with those around us; it expresses our need for forgiveness and our desire to receive it from our sisters and brothers. Reconciliation with them prepares us for Communion, as we receive the Body and Blood of Christ given up for us. This is not a private, solitary affair. Unity with Christ's Eucharistic Body brings communion with his Mystical Body. When we say amen to the Body of Christ, it is an amen to him but also to all who are joined with him. The *Catechism* tells us, quite explicitly, that the Eucharist directs our concern toward the poor. We must recognize Christ in the poorest of his brothers and sisters (see #1397).

The *Concluding Rites.* After a period of contemplative reflection, the Eucharist quickly concludes with a final prayer, a blessing and a sending forth of the community to live what it has celebrated. The gathered community becomes once again the scattered community, as people strive to live the gospel in the many ways of life to which God has called them.

The Sunday, the Lord's Day, will come again, and once

more the people of the community will respond to my young friend's question: "What time is Church?"

Growing in Knowledge

1) Why are there so many names for the Eucharist?

2) What are the two meanings of memorial in Scripture?

3) How is the Eucharist a sacrifice?

Growing in Faith

1) Describe what the Eucharist means to you.

2) What is your most memorable experience of Eucharist?

3) Name some ways to connect your daily life to Sunday Eucharist.

CHAPTER SEVEN

The Sacraments of Healing: Reconciliation and the Anointing of the Sick

> *Thus, just as the sacraments of Baptism, Confirmation, and the Eucharist form a unity called "the sacraments of Christian initiation," so too it can be said that Penance, the Anointing of the Sick and the Eucharist as viaticum constitute at the end of Christian life "the sacraments that prepare for our heavenly homeland" or the sacraments that complete our earthly pilgrimage.*—Catechism of the Catholic Church, #1525

Saint Jerome, so the story goes, once had a vision in which Christ spoke to him: "There is something I want you to give me." Jerome, who at the time was living in a cave in Bethlehem, replied in a rather hurt tone, "I have given up everything for you. What can you possibly want from me?" "Give me your sins," Christ said, "so that I may forgive them."

The story may not be historical truth, but its message rings true. It tells us two things: First, no matter how close we may be to God, the reality of sin is something we all experience. We know firsthand the mystifying paradox of the human condition of which Paul speaks: "I do not understand my own actions. For I do not do what I want, but I do the very thing I hate.... For I do not do the good I want, but the evil I do not want is what I do" (Romans 7:15, 19). We can all identify with Paul's bewilderment at what is going on inside him. Like him, we ask ourselves about our actions. In honest bewilderment we say to ourselves: "Why in the world did I do that? Why did I say that?"

There is an orneriness about us, a lack of freedom that we cannot overcome simply by ourselves. We realize that we are sinners. We know that we need the help of God's grace.

The second truth which the Jerome story tells us is that the grace of God is always available to us. God is eager to forgive our sins. This is what Jesus meant when he said that "there will be more joy in heaven over one sinner who repents than over ninety-nine righteous persons who need no repentance" (Luke 15:7). These words are embedded in a chapter that has three marvelous parables about God's love for sinners: The Lost Sheep, The Lost Coin and The Lost Son (The Prodigal Son). In these three parables Jesus reveals to us the depths of God's mercy and love.

We must not forget that Jesus told these striking parables in response to the grumbling of Pharisees and scribes who were upset that Jesus welcomed sinners and ate with them. Jesus dared to tell them: The way I act is the way God acts. Jesus incarnated the love of God in his person and in his actions (#1443).

This chapter deals with the sacraments of healing: Reconciliation and the Anointing of the Sick. Any discussion of these sacraments must be against the background of two important realities: (1) our sense of our own sinfulness, and (2) the incredible, wondrous reality of God's mighty love and God's eagerness to forgive us our sins.

The Sacrament of Reconciliation

The power to forgive sin Christ gave to the Church has been exercised in a variety of ways through the centuries (see #1447). A variety of names has emphasized different aspects of the sacrament at different times (#1423-1424). It has been called the Sacrament of Conversion because it ritualizes the first step (the turning around) one must take to return to God. "Sacrament of Penance" places primary emphasis on the satisfaction or penance that one is given in the sacrament.

"Confession" was common when the stress seemed to be on telling one's sins and submitting them for forgiveness. "The Sacrament of Pardon" focuses on the fruit of the sacrament: the pardon and peace that God gives.

The dominant name today is the Sacrament of Reconciliation. This is an especially appropriate designation; it indicates that our communion with God and with one another is restored or deepened. For *reconciliation* means making one what was separated or deepening a superficial oneness. Reconciliation removes the barriers that cause separation or prevent deep union. The sacrament celebrates both horizontal reconciliation (with our sisters and brothers) and vertical reconciliation (with God). It always involves conversion, that is, a turning toward the other (#1468-1470).

Jesus stressed the need of horizontal reconciliation when he admonished us that reconciliation with our brother or sister was a prerequisite for offering our gifts to God at the altar: "So when you are offering your gift at the altar, if you remember that your brother or sister has something against you, leave your gift there before the altar and go; first be reconciled to your brother or sister, and then come and offer your gift" (Matthew 5:23-24).

Reconciliation with God is what Paul sees God doing among us. "...[I]n Christ God was reconciling the world to himself...and entrusting the message of reconciliation to us.... [W]e entreat you on behalf of Christ, be reconciled to God" (2 Corinthians 5:19a, 20b).

Jesus carefully linked the horizontal and vertical aspects of reconciliation in the parable of the Unforgiving Servant (Matthew 18:31-35). Himself forgiven much, the servant refused to forgive a fellow-servant. Jesus makes clear the close connection between our forgiving others and our ability to receive God's forgiveness. This fundamental truth is enshrined in the Lord's Prayer, where we ask that we be forgiven to the degree that we ourselves forgive.

I recall a moving story told by a wonderful peacemaker, Hildegard Goss-Mayr of Vienna, Austria. After the Second World War, she made a visit to Warsaw with a peace group. One evening, meeting in secrecy with a number of Polish families, she told them that she had come from a group of Christian Germans. They wanted to come to Warsaw to ask the pardon of these Polish people for the atrocities that Germany had inflicted upon their homeland. One of the Poles cried out: "No, Hildegard, we cannot receive them. The streets of Warsaw flowed with blood. To ask us to forgive this is asking too much."

She did not push the issue any further. But as she was leaving the meeting, she suggested that all pray the Lord's Prayer. When they came to the words, "Forgive us, as we forgive...," they stopped. There was a pause.

Then one of them said: "We understand what you are asking for. Yes, we must forgive them."

Why Post-Baptismal Reconciliation?

The sacraments of initiation bring new life in Christ, but that life takes full possession of us only gradually. We have to struggle with the weaknesses and frailties that are part of the human condition. We are not yet fully attuned to the promptings of God's Spirit. We can misuse our freedom and sin. After the first and fundamental conversion of Baptism, we must experience other conversions as slowly, gradually, sometimes painfully, sometimes joyfully, we move ahead toward the fullness of new life in Christ. As the *Catechism* puts it, "Christ's call to conversion continues to resound in the lives of Christians" (#1428). Conversion is thus an ongoing task. Ours is the continuing story of a Church that is holy because of its union with Christ and yet, at the same time, is always in need of purification from all those forces which obscure that union. Such purification is both an individual task and a community responsibility. It calls for penance and renewal.

A Change of Heart (#1430-1439)

Conversion is not just a series of external actions. It involves above all else a change of heart, a radical reorientation of our lives from within.

> Yet even now, says the LORD,
> return to me with all your heart...;

rend your hearts and not your clothing.
Return to the LORD, your God.... (Joel 2:12a, 13a)

Jesus stood in this prophetic tradition when, replying to criticism for associating with sinners, he said to his detractors: "Go and learn what this means, 'I desire mercy, not sacrifice' " (Matthew 9:13a). Rooted in a contrite and humble heart, conversion can express itself in many ways in daily life: for example, making sincere efforts at reconciliation with our sisters and brothers, admitting our offenses against others, caring for the poor, defending right and justice, working for peace, that active love of others that "covers a multitude of sins" (see 1 Peter 4:8). The season of Lent and the observance of Friday abstinence in memory of the Lord's death are privileged moments in the Christian journey of penance and conversion.

The Sacramental Rite

History (#1440-1449). During his public ministry Jesus forgave sin and showed his desire to forgive by the table fellowship he shared with people who were looked upon as sinners. By sharing his power to forgive sin with the apostles, Jesus gave them the power to reconcile sinners. The authority of binding (excluding from communion with the Church) and loosing (receiving back into that communion) is a power ratified by God (see Matthew 16:19; 18:18).

The specific forms this sacrament has taken have varied considerably. During the early centuries, great emphasis was placed on *rigorous public penance* imposed upon people who were guilty of serious public sins (such as apostasy, murder or adultery). By the fourth century such people were enrolled in the order of penitents. They might be required to do penance for a number of years before receiving reconciliation. In the seventh century Irish monks, inspired by the Egyptian monastic tradition, began celebrating the sacrament in a more private way. This developed into the form of the sacrament (confessor and individual penitent meeting, generally, in anonymity) that prevailed until the Second Vatican Council introduced three rites.

Beneath the changes, we can see a fundamental structure: on the one hand, the actions of the penitent; on the other, God's action through the mediation of the Church.

Acts of the Penitent (#1450-1460). Three acts of the penitent are involved. The first is *contrition*, sorrow for sin coupled with the determination to avoid it in the future. The second is *confession*, an admission of our sins and a willingness to take responsibility for them. By sorrow and confession one disowns sin. The *Catechism* quotes Saint Augustine, who speaks of confession as "destroying sin." Distinguishing between the person—"what God has made"—and what the person has made, he admonishes: "Destroy what you have made, so that God may save what he has made" (#1458).

The third action of the penitent is *satisfaction*: something to atone for his or her sins. It is also referred to as a "penance." It is intended to be healing, not punitive: it should help us to become more like Christ. We need to remember, though, that Christ has already made atonement for our sins; because of him we are able to achieve at-one-ment with God.

Absolution (#1449). In the early Church absolution and the penitent's return to full communion with the Church *followed* the satisfaction; now it normally *precedes* it. The sacramental formula actually combines two forms of absolution: one intercessory and one declaratory. It refers to God, the Father of mercies, the Paschal Mystery of God's Son, the gift of the Spirit and the ministry of the Church.

> God, the Father of mercies,
> through the death and resurrection of his Son
> has reconciled the world to himself
> and sent the Holy Spirit among us
> for the forgiveness of sins;
> through the ministry of the Church
> may God give you pardon and peace,
> and I absolve you from your sins
> in the name of the Father and of the Son and of the Holy Spirit.

The Celebration of the Sacrament
The modern rites are intended to make the sacrament more evidently an ecclesial event. After the priest greets the penitent (face-to-face or through a screen) they share an appropriate reading from the Word of God, calling the penitent to reconciliation. After reflection, the penitent reveals his or her sins. The confessor assigns a penance, offers counsel and gives absolution; the penitent says a prayer of repentance and praise. The entire rite is intended to be a joyful celebration of God's goodness in forgiving us our sins.

In addition to this rite of individual reconciliation are two other rites of a communal nature. One calls for individual confession and absolution in the context of a Scripture service. A second form calls also for a full celebration of the word of God, but includes communal confession and absolution. The present discipline of the Church allows this last of the three rites only in cases of urgent necessity.

The Anointing of the Sick (#1499-1513)

Illness can lead to self-absorption, despair, even rebellion against God. But it can also strengthen people and bring a calm and peaceful acceptance of the inevitable. The *Catechism* reminds us that in every illness we catch a glimpse of death (see #1500). Every illness is a diminishment that points inevitably to life's end.

While we should do what we can to combat illness and prudently seek the blessings of good health, we must at the same time be prepared, to use the mysterious words of Saint Paul, to make up in our own person "what is lacking in Christ's afflictions" (see Colossians 1:24). The sick have an important ministry in the Church: to witness to the frailty of human life and to the deeper, lasting realities of human existence.

Christ's compassion brought healing to many during his life on earth; he identified himself with the sick (see Matthew 25:36). His disciples must imitate his love for the sick. The centuries pay eloquent witness to Christians' dedication to the care of the sick and the dying. Everywhere the Church has built and staffed hospitals to care for the ill and the afflicted.

More than that, the Church has a sacrament to bring comfort, strength and peace to those who are being tested by illness, attested to by Saint James: the Anointing of the Sick.

> Are any among you sick? They should call for the elders [*presbyters*] of the church and have them pray over them, anointing them with oil in the name of the Lord. The prayer of faith will save the sick, and the Lord will raise them up; and anyone who has committed sins will be forgiven. (James 5:14-15)

Note that James does not speak of those "at the point of death," but simply those who are "sick." This means that when any of the faithful begin to be endangered by sickness or old age, they may fittingly receive this sacrament (#1514-1516).

Celebration of the Sacrament (#1517-1525)

Like all the sacraments, the Anointing of the Sick is a community liturgy. Depending on the circumstances, it may take place in home, hospital or church. It is appropriately celebrated during the Eucharist.

The liturgy begins with a Penitential Rite, followed by a Liturgy of the Word. The priest prays over and lays hands on the sick person, and anoints him or her with the oil of the sick (blessed by the bishop on Holy Thursday).

The principal effect of the sacrament is to give the comfort, peace and courage needed to face the difficulties that come with serious illness or the frailty of old age. People's sins are forgiven and they are united to Christ's Passion. In a sense, they participate in his saving work and thus contribute to the sanctification of the whole Church. "The Anointing of the Sick," in the words of the *Catechism*, "completes our conformity to the death and Resurrection of Christ, just as Baptism began it" (#1523).

Viaticum: The Christian's Last Sacrament

The last sacrament of a Christian life is not the Anointing of the Sick, but viaticum: Communion received at the moment of "passover" to God.

Baptism, Confirmation and the Eucharist initiated us into the community of the faithful, as participation in the Eucharist throughout our lives sustained us in the ongoing journey of that community. So Reconciliation, Anointing and the Eucharist as viaticum bring our earthly pilgrimage to a close and prepare us for the fullness of life in God.

GROWING IN KNOWLEDGE

1) What are the three fundamental acts of the penitent?

2) How did Vatican II change the Rite of Reconciliation?

3) What important ministry do the sick perform?

4) What is the principal effect of the Sacrament of Anointing?

GROWING IN FAITH

1) Describe an experience of reconciliation in your life.

2) How do you experience ongoing conversion?

3) Would you rather celebrate a healing sacrament in private or in a group? Why?

4) When has the Sacrament of Reconciliation most been an experience of healing for you?

CHAPTER EIGHT

Sacraments in the Service of Community: Holy Orders and Matrimony

> *Holy Orders and Matrimony...confer a particular mission in the Church and serve to build up the People of God.*—Catechism of the Catholic Church, #1534

In 1808 Napoleon captured Rome and imprisoned Pope Pius VII. One day, in a stormy meeting with the pope, the emperor said to him: "I am going to destroy this Church of yours." The pope laughed at him and said: "We clergy have been trying to do that for 1800 years. We haven't succeeded. Neither will you."

Holy Orders

The encounter between pope and emperor may seem a rather disheartening way of introducing the Sacrament of Holy Orders. Yet in recent times moral lapses on the part of some priests and bishops have gained publicity too wide to ignore.

The *Catechism* states quite plainly that bishops and priests are not immune from human weaknesses, from the spirit of domination, error and sin (#1550). Still, this dark side of the Church's hierarchical structure must not be allowed to overshadow the dedication and commitment of the countless bishops and priests who have given their lives wholeheartedly in the service of God's Kingdom. For every one whose life casts doubts on the credibility of the Church structure, there are many, many whose life and work continue to make the message of the gospel believable in today's world. The lapses of the few cannot be allowed to eclipse the dedication of the many.

'Orders' (#1533-1538)

The term *orders* was apparently influenced by the Letter to the Hebrews, which speaks of Christ as a priest "according to the order of Melchizedek" in contrast to priesthood "according to the order of Aaron" (see Hebrews 7:11). In each case the word expresses some kind of divine arrangement that relates one in a special way to the service of God.

Actually, the word *order* is not uncommon in Church vocabulary. In its most general sense it means an organization of persons or things or actions directed toward some sacred purpose. Thus we speak of the "order of catechumens" into which we enroll those who are preparing for the sacraments of initiation. The "order of penitents" described public sinners who were preparing themselves through penitential acts for return to full communion with the Church. The "order of the Mass" clarifies the rituals to be followed in the celebration of the Eucharist. "Holy Orders" (plural, because there are several ranks) refers to the body that gives leadership and direction to the community of faith.

During the first century the leadership of the Church went through a process of development whose stages, for lack of adequate evidence, remain somewhat obscure. By the dawn of the second century, what we now call the Sacrament of Orders consisted of bishops, priests (presbyters) and deacons, all empowered by God to exercise authority in the Church for the service of the whole people of God, each according to his own rank.

A Priestly People (#1539-1553)

The history of Israel offers something of a parallel to developments in Christianity. All Israel was established as a priestly people, but one of the tribes, Levi, was chosen to minister to the people and represent them before God. In a similar fashion, through the sacraments of initiation, all Christians share in the priestly role of Christ; a common priesthood belongs to all. But even a priestly community (the

Church as well as ancient Israel) needs some kind of governance and some source of instruction. Moreover, the community of Christ's followers needs to have the sacrificial act of Christ's sanctifying love made present. To govern, to teach, to lead in worship—these are the divinely appointed tasks of the ministerial or hierarchical priesthood.

In other words, bishops, priests and deacons are chosen from among the chosen to represent and to serve all the chosen. They are, as it were, the elect among the elect. This does not give them a dignity greater than the rest of the people. It *does* give them a special role to exercise on behalf of God's people and divine empowerment to carry out that role. For this reason the *Catechism*, quoting Vatican II, states that the ministerial or hierarchical priesthood and the common priesthood of all the faithful differ *in essence, not only in degree*. Still, they also remain interrelated, for both participate, "each in its own proper way, in the one priesthood of Christ" (#1547).

The *Constitution on the Church* made this even more explicit: "The distinction which the Lord made between sacred ministers and the rest of the people of God entails a unifying purpose, since pastors and the other faithful are bound to each other by a mutual need. Pastors of the Church, following the example of the Lord, should minister to one another and to the other faithful. The faithful in their turn should enthusiastically lend their cooperative assistance to their pastors and teachers" (#32).

There was a time when *ordination* meant entrance into any order. Thus one could speak of being ordained a catechumen. Today the term is reserved for that sacramental act whereby a man is introduced into the orders of the episcopate, the presbyterate or the diaconate (#1538).

Though there are three ranks in Holy Orders, only the first two are priestly. Deacons are ordained, but they are not priests. Their role is to help and serve the two other orders. The Latin word for priest, *sacerdos*, is applied only to bishops and priests.

The Order of Bishops (#1554-1561)

Catholic tradition from earliest times gives pride of place among the various ministries in the Church to the bishop.

Bishops, the successors of the apostles, "bear the apostolic seed," as the *Constitution on the Church* puts it (#20; see *Catechism*, #1555). Bishops possess the fullness of the Sacrament of Orders. Through the laying on of hands and the prayer of consecration, episcopal ordination confers the power to teach, govern and sanctify in a local Church. It likewise brings participation in the college of bishops with the Bishop of Rome as their head.

For many centuries bishops were chosen by their local Church. Today lawful ordination of a bishop requires appointment by the pope. This became necessary in the eleventh century, when secular rulers were often choosing unworthy bishops. The pope was the only power strong enough at that time to oppose and prevent the choice of bishops by a country's ruler. The power of appointment now exercised by the Bishop of Rome does not mean that bishops of local Churches are delegates of the Roman pontiff or his vicars. The bishops' authority comes from God through their episcopal consecration.

Each bishop, therefore, is vicar of Christ in the local Church entrusted to him. But his vision cannot simply be turned inward, for he also shares collegially with his brother bishops, under the leadership of the Bishop of Rome, a concern for all the Churches.

The celebration of the Eucharist by the local bishop, with his presbyters and the rest of the faithful gathered about him, is of special importance. It mirrors the Church in its fullness. Saint Ignatius of Antioch wrote: "Where the bishop is, there is the Church."

The Order of Priests (#1562-1568)

Though they do not possess the fullness of the priesthood and are subordinate to the bishop in the exercise of their priestly power, priests (presbyters) are called to cooperate with the bishop. United with him in one priestly college, they help to serve the needs of the people of the local Church. Thus collegiality is understood not only as bishops of local Churches working with one another, but also as priests in a particular local Church sharing with the bishop the priestly ministry to all the faithful. Priests are empowered, in subordination to the bishop, to act in the person of Christ, the Head of the Church.

In recent years there has been much discussion regarding the role of the priest. The *Catechism* suggests three responsibilities to which priests are called. The first is to proclaim the gospel. This is a duty which makes various demands. It includes preaching homilies, instructing people, reaching out with the gospel message to those who have never heard it and to those who have heard it but rejected it. Proclaiming the gospel must be done with the boldness and courage engendered by the message and at the same time with a sensitivity and proper concern for those to whom the proclamation is directed.

The second responsibility of the priest is to shepherd the faithful. What this entails will vary markedly with the situation in which the priest exercises his ministry. It surely includes availability and willingness to listen, genuine concern and love for people, eagerness to empower all the faithful in their proper ministries, a sense of compassion, a sincere and dedicated commitment to the needs of the poor, the lonely, the oppressed.

The third responsibility of the priest is to celebrate the sacred mysteries with the faithful. Liturgy ritualizes the faith life of a community. A priest who presides at liturgy with a prayerful spirit that embodies care and joy, a sense of the human and of the holy, will enhance the faith of the community.

The Order of Deacons (#1569-1571)

Deacons are ordained for the Church's ministry of service. Though they do not receive the ministerial priesthood, ordination confers on them important functions: proclaiming and preaching the word of God, assisting the bishop and priests in liturgy, especially at the Eucharist, distributing Communion, witnessing and blessing weddings and participating in the Church's various ministries of charity.

For a long time the diaconate was the next-to-last step toward the priesthood. It had become a transitional stage toward priestly ordination. No one was ordained to remain a deacon. On the recommendation of the bishops of the Second

Vatican Council, the diaconate has been restored as a permanent order in the Church. It is the one order that admits married candidates.

The Celebration of the Sacrament (#1575-1591)

The bishop is the minister of Orders. Only baptized men may be ordained, and normally they must be willing to observe celibacy for the sake of the Kingdom. Priests are called to a life of ongoing conversion that will enable them to be fruitful ministers of the Kingdom of God. Saint Gregory Nazianzen, as a very young priest, exclaimed: "We must begin by purifying ourselves before purifying others; we must be instructed to be able to instruct, become light to illuminate, draw close to God to bring him close to others..." (#1589).

The Sacrament of Matrimony

There has been much talk in recent years about the need to establish base communities within the context of larger parish units. The need springs from the anonymity that so easily settles over a large congregation.

In a sense, there have always been base communities in the Church: the families of a parish. Indeed, the Christian home has been called the *ecclesiola*, the little Church. Marriage is God's plan for bringing such small communities into existence.

Marriage in God's Plan (#1601-1617)

Marriage has been a very different institution at various times and in various cultures. Yet a sense of its importance exists everywhere. For man and woman were created by God to image in their mutual love the divine love that gave them being.

The Genesis narrative makes clear that man and woman were made as equal partners to live in intimacy with one another, an intimacy so close that they become one flesh. Jesus speaks of the permanency of this intimate union when he speaks of the Creator's plan from the beginning: "So they are no longer two, but one flesh" (Matthew 19:6a).

The Book of Genesis also describes the rupture and

distortion of the mutual communion between the man and the woman. The harmony of paradise was lost and the original communion of man and woman often degenerated into recrimination, manipulation, dominance and lust. The universality of this disruption of human relationship is the result of what we name "original sin," the condition in which people are born and which they are unable to escape from except through the redemptive grace brought by Jesus Christ.

Jesus' presence at the wedding at Cana is the sign that he confirms the original goodness of the marriage relationship. More than that, in his preaching he teaches unequivocally the original meaning of the marriage covenant and God's will that it be indissoluble. Jesus' coming to restore all of creation to its initial order includes the call to married people to accept his saving grace and thus receive the power to restore marriage to its innate goodness. Christ, our savior, comes as the Bridegroom to reclaim his bride, the Church. Christian marriage is a sacrament, a true sign of the spousal relationship of Christ with his Church. The ideal of marriage, as Christ expressed it, was not the bill of divorce sanctioned by Moses, but an indissoluble union: "Therefore what God has joined together, let no one separate" (Matthew 19:6b).

The Celebration of Marriage (#1621-1642)

The celebration of marriage between two Catholics normally takes place during Mass. Since the Eucharist is the memorial of the new covenant of Christ's gift of himself for his beloved bride, the Church, it is fitting that spouses seal their covenant with one another by uniting themselves and their mutual love with his eucharistic sacrifice and sharing the communion of his Body and Blood in the midst of the Christian community.

The spouses are ministers of grace to one another. They confer the sacrament on each other by expressing their consent before the Christian community.

Marriage preparation is of the greatest importance. It can help to guarantee that the exchange of consent will be a free and responsible act. Those best qualified to conduct such marriage preparation courses are married couples who have known firsthand the joys and trials of married life, who have the wisdom that comes from experience and the ability to articulate that experience. Practical principles that can enhance human relationships, peaceful ways of resolving conflicts and guidelines for dealing with children are all part of the human dimension of married life together. The spirituality of married and family life needs to be explored in terms of the universal call to holiness expressed by Vatican II.

The *Catechism* speaks of mixed marriages (marriages between Catholics and baptized non-Catholics) and also of marriages between persons of different religions (where one is not baptized). While warning against the dangers involved in such marriages, especially the latter, the *Catechism* makes clear that difference of religious affiliation need not be "an insurmountable obstacle to marriage" (#1634). Sharing through dialogue what each has received from his or her religious tradition can be a learning experience for both and can deepen the Catholic's own commitment to Christ. The *Catechism* also encourages ecumenical efforts at marriage preparation where there is difference of religious affiliation. This can encourage the development of what unites the couple and respect for what still separates them.

The Purposes of Marriage (#2360-2378)

Avoiding the pre-Vatican II distinction that spoke of the primary and secondary purposes of marriage, the *Catechism* speaks of its twofold end: the good of the spouses and the transmission of life (#2363). This means that married life requires both fidelity (for the good of the spouses) and openness to life. The *Catechism*, following the teaching of *Humanae Vitae*, Pope Paul VI's encyclical on birth control, goes a step beyond linking fidelity and openness to life. It insists that this openness to life must apply to every conjugal act. In the words of the encyclical: "each and every marriage act must remain open to the transmission of life" (#2366, see *Humanae Vitae*, #11). One does not have to read very far in newspapers and magazines, both Catholic and secular, to realize that there are those—many by no means rebellious toward Church authority—who wish that the encyclical had called for an openness to life in marriage as a whole rather than in "each and every marriage act." This was the position recommended by a large majority of the Commission on birth control set up by Pope John XXIII and expanded by Pope Paul VI. After two years of deliberating on their findings, Pope Paul VI felt obliged to reject their recommendations and reaffirm his predecessor's position.

The *Catechism* follows the teaching of *Humanae Vitae* in its teaching on responsible parenthood. Avoiding conception is justifiable if it does not proceed from selfish reasons and if it does not resort to any sort of action "which either before, during or after intercourse, is specifically intended to prevent procreation—whether as an end or as a means" (*Humanae Vitae*, #14). Such actions are declared "intrinsically evil." Periodic continence, methods of birth control based on self-observation and the use of infertile periods conform, the *Catechism* says, to objective criteria of morality and are therefore permissible.

The Domestic Church (1655-1658)

The fruitfulness of marriage involves parents not only in begetting children, but also in their moral, spiritual and ecclesial upbringing. Education begins in the home. Parents are always the first and most important teachers of their children: in faith, in morality, in learning to be more and more fully human and Christian. In this domestic Church worship as well as education takes place. In family prayer and through participation in the sacramental life of the Church, parents and children exercise the priesthood of the baptized. In the domestic Church the real presence of Christ can be experienced. "For," he said, "where two or three are gathered in my name, I am there among them" (Matthew 18:20).

Reflections on marriage and the values it offers to Church and society must not lead us to forget the large number of persons who are single, either by choice or by circumstances over which they have no control. They too are called to live lives of sincere spiritual dedication to Christ, to the Church and to the poor. Some live the life of simplicity expressed in the Beatitudes. Others live in poverty and homelessness. All such persons must be embraced in love and concern by both the domestic Church and the wider Church.

GROWING IN KNOWLEDGE

1) What sacrament underlies both Holy Orders and Matrimony?

2) How does ordained ministry differ from the priesthood of all believers?

3) Why do we call Christian marriage a sacrament?

GROWING IN FAITH

1) How have you shared in the priesthood of Christ?

2) What is the most challenging aspect of your vocation?

3) How is your home the domestic Church? How can you make it more evidently so?

CHAPTER NINE

Love: The Basis of Christian Morality

> *Each of us must be sufficiently present to ourselves to hear and follow the voice of conscience. This demand for* inwardness *(interiority) is the more pressing, given that life often deprives us of opportunities for reflection, examination and self-awareness.—See* Catechism of the Catholic Church, #1779

In 1956 Cecil B. De Mille produced his famous movie, *The Ten Commandments*, a remake of an earlier (1923) film on the same subject. Those who have seen this movie will remember the dramatic way in which the Ten Commandments are given by God: engraved on rock tablets in huge characters by an invisible hand that writes with fiery darts of lightning.

I don't recall whether the movie shows the people being prepared to receive the Commandments or whether they were thrust unexpected upon a hapless and frightened people. But the *Catechism* does prepare readers for the Commandments.

Preparing to Study the Commandments

Part III of *Catechism of the Catholic Church* is generally described as dealing with the Ten Commandments. It would perhaps be better to say that it is about Christian morality or about the moral life of the Christian. Nowhere is its difference from the Council of Trent's *Roman Catechism* more pronounced than in this section. The latter moves from a study of the Sacrament of Matrimony directly into the Decalogue, the

Ten Commandments. The new *Catechism* departs from this procedure, preparing its readers for the Commandments in two ways.

First, it places the presentation of the Ten Commandments in the context of the twofold command of love: love of God, subject of the first three, and love of neighbor, the concern of the remaining seven (#2052-2055). Thus the Commandments, which include a number of "thou shalt nots," are cast in a more positive context. While in no way mitigating the importance of the things we need to avoid (murder, adultery, stealing and so on), the *Catechism* offers love as the motive that should prompt our avoidance.

The *Catechism* also prepares us to study the Commandments by speaking about general issues involving our moral life: the acting persons involved in keeping the commands of love. In #1691-2051 it speaks about the communities to which we belong and in which we exercise responsibility. It discusses the morality of human actions, the meaning of conscience, virtue and vice. It clarifies the new law of the gospel and the role of the Church in teaching about moral matters. By the time we get to the Commandments, we have the necessary moral equipment at hand to deal with the issues raised by them.

The Way to Happiness

Christ called himself the Way, the Truth and the Life (see John 14:6). If we think of Part I of the *Catechism* (a study of the Creed) as presenting Christ, the Truth, and Part II (a discussion of the sacramental signs of Christ's presence among us) as Christ, the Life, Parts Three and Four (on the moral and spiritual life of the Christian) could be thought of as Christ, the Way.

The way of Christ is the way of the Beatitudes and the way to beatitude. Happiness (what *beatitude* means) is the destiny God has in store for us. That happiness has been variously described. In universal terms it is called the coming of God's Kingdom; more personally, it is described as the vision of God.

Happiness is the realization of one's identity, an identity that is found only in God. To put it in biblical terms, it is the *image of God recovering the likeness of God.* The image of God is to be found in our humanity. Our likeness of God means communion with God.

The Image and Likeness of God

The Book of Genesis offers a story which shows the difference between image and likeness. It tells us that the man and woman were made *in the image and likeness of God.* This likeness, their communion with God, is beautifully portrayed as walking with God in the cool evening breezes. This picture of joy and happiness quickly gives way to a very different scene: one of misery and gloom. Instead of walking with God, the man and woman hide themselves. Sin has entered the world. Some of the Church Fathers understood the Genesis story of sin to mean the loss of the *likeness* of God. The *image* of God remained, but only the coming of Christ and his Spirit makes possible the recovery of likeness to God, which constitutes happiness.

Reason (#1702-1782). The image of God is present in every person (see #1702). That image includes reason, free will and human emotions. By reason we come to know "the order of things established by the Creator" (#1704). We can grow in knowledge and deepen our understanding.

Freedom. By our free will (the outstanding sign of the divine image in us; see #1705), we can seek and love the true and the good. And "the more one does what is good, the freer one becomes." For freedom fundamentally consists not in the power to choose good or evil, but freely to choose the good. For to choose evil is a misuse of freedom: one becomes a slave to that evil. The only true freedom is the choice of what is good (#1733).

The *Virtues.* We experience pleasure, desire, aversion, surprise, hope, joy, fear and so on. Emotions can affect—limit or enhance—our freedom and thus modify the moral character of what we do. Our emotions can be fashioned into virtues that make it easier for us to choose the good, or they can be perverted into vices that incline us to turn away from the good.

Four virtues play a pivotal role in the Christian life. Called the *cardinal virtues* (*cardo* in Latin means "hinge"), they are prudence, which moves us to make wise choices habitually; justice, the steadfast will to give to God and neighbor their due; fortitude, stability in seeking the good even in the face of difficulties; temperance, which moderates and balances our uses of created things and keeps our desires within proper limits (#1805-1810).

There are also the theological virtues, which accompany God's gift of grace: faith, whereby we commit our lives to God and assent to God's self-revelation; hope, the confident trust founded not on our efforts but on the promises of Christ that we shall attain happiness; and love, which enables us to fulfill with joy the twofold command of loving God above all things and our neighbor as ourselves.

Love is the virtue that binds all the others together. Saint Thomas Aquinas called it the "form" of all the virtues. Saint Paul speaks of love as binding "everything together in perfect harmony" (see Colossians 3:14). It is also the goal of the Christian life. For ultimately it is love that unites us with God and enables us to find ourselves in God (#1812-1845).

Inner Unity

By our efforts to live the virtues we gradually build up our moral character. We cultivate an inner unity that gives consistency and stability to our persons and to the actions we perform. The more we create this inner unity in ourselves, the less haphazard and unpredictable will our actions be (#1779).

It is in building this moral unity that we form our consciences. Conscience is recognizing God's voice speaking to us in the depths of our being. As the *Catechism* says, quoting Vatican II, "Conscience is a person's most intimate core and sanctuary where he or she is alone with God, whose voice resounds within" (#1776).

The voice of God in the depths of our being, calling us to true happiness, is challenged at times by the sinful instincts in us, which urge us to misuse our freedom and choose behavior that is ultimately destructive and hurtful to ourselves and to the society in which we live.

This is what morality is all about: the decisions we make as we hear the call of God, yet experience, at the same time, the pull of sinful instincts that have somehow become a part of who we are. As the *Catechism* puts it: All Christian morality rests on this call to beatitude, which challenges us "with decisive moral choices. It invites us to purify our hearts of bad instincts and to seek the love of God above all else." Christian morality "teaches us that true happiness is not found in riches or well-being, in human fame or power, or in any human achievement—however beneficial it may be—such as science, technology, and art, or indeed in any creature, but in God alone, the source of every good and of all love" (#1723).

This is not to belittle human efforts, but only to refuse to give them priority. The Second Vatican Council, while warning of the danger of gaining the whole world and losing one's true self in the process, does say that our expectation of ultimate happiness does not weaken our concern for the needs of this life, "for it is here that the body of a new human family grows, foreshadowing in some way the age which is to come" (*The Church in the Modern World*, #39). That is why an important aspect of Christian morality is to work for peace, justice and harmony in society: to create a human atmosphere in which people can make wise moral decisions and respond to God's call to happiness.

Freedom and Conscience (#1730-1742; 1776-1782)

Our freedom opens our inner ears to the voice of God in the call of conscience. Freedom is the power of self-determination, which sets humans apart from other created beings. Humans do not exist harnessed, as it were, to a natural order which totally determines their natures. A plant or animal becomes what it is by nature. As a poet says: "Snails obey the will of God slowly." A human being, on the other hand, is open to various possibilities of self-realization. We are not predetermined by some internal compulsion over which we have no control to achieve a certain type of personhood. We have—obviously within certain limits of nature and grace—the power to become the person we will to be.

Our freedom to become ourselves is historically situated: We strive to become ourselves in the context of a particular set of historical circumstances and of interrelationships with other persons. Historical circumstances may help or impede our personal growth. The persons we meet may open or close themselves to us and thus limit or enhance the scope of our freedom and its exercise.

Conscience involves not only a unique expression of our freedom; it also begets responsibility. In fact, we could say that conscience is the experience of responsibility in the exercise of our freedom. *Responsibility* is a tricky word. There is a certain ambiguity about it. Used in a passive sense, it means "accountability," that I am held responsible for what I do. In a more active sense, *responsibility* means that I am acting in a responsible way.

But the fact that I am responsible (accountable) for my actions does not necessarily make me a responsible person. The person who drives way beyond the speed limit on a crowded street is accountable for any accidents this reckless drive may cause. Yet he or she can hardly be called a "responsible" person. There are times when I may be held responsible for behavior that is irresponsible.

Responsibility, in its active meaning, means "*responsiveness*." I am called to be responsive to the moral demands of the situation in which I find myself. I must be responsive to the values that exist in that situation, to the law of my nature, to the challenges of gospel values as understood in the Church community, to the inspirations of the indwelling Spirit who reveals in the depths of my consciousness the demands of the all-embracing law of love.

This is why conscience is described as "the most secret core and sanctuary of a person" where the person is alone with God, whose voice echoes in the soul's depths. This voice reveals that law which is fulfilled by love of God and neighbor (#1776; see *The Church in the Modern World*, #1).

The Formation of Conscience (#1783-1801)

Catechists have the responsibility to help those whom they

teach to develop sound and mature consciences. This means that catechists and religious instructors must communicate the moral doctrines taught by the magisterium of the Church and held by the Christian community. At the same time they must encourage people to think for themselves. These two endeavors must go hand in hand. Only if people are given a knowledge of moral truth can thinking for themselves be responsible. But it is equally true to say that only if they are thinking for themselves will the moral doctrine communicated to them become convictions personally held by them. For there is a huge difference between convictions that I personally assent to and unassimilated knowledge that I have received but never made my own. We have to invite people to examine critically what they believe, not with a view to rejecting it, but rather with a view to assimilating it and making it their own. Without this personal appropriation of what they have been taught, these truths will not be a vital influence in their decisions. Often a moral crisis under which they break reveals how superficial their moral commitments actually were.

It is important, too, to communicate a sense of joy in the living of the Christian life. Our moral life must not be seen as the price we have to pay to save our souls, but rather as a joyful response to the God who created us out of love and whose love calls us to happiness—not just in the next life, but in this life also. This is not to deny that this life does have its sorrows and heartaches (more for some people than for others). The circumstances that create such situations are not always under our control. Yet whatever our trials, we can, ordinarily and by God's grace, find a good measure of happiness even in this anteroom to eternal life.

Person and Community (#1787-1927)

Up to now, we have talked about human beings, their dignity, their moral life, their freedom and responsibility and how conscience experiences responsibility in the exercise of freedom. But we can never ignore the fact that persons live in community. As members of the human community, we have responsibilities toward others. Indeed, it is through reaction and interaction with persons in community that we use our gifts and become most fully who we are.

At this point it would be helpful to recall the twofold meaning of "responsibility" described above: that is, both accountability and responsiveness. The latter especially brings a certain creativity into our moral lives.

Thomas Merton, who died near the end of the stormy sixties in 1968, wrote in 1966:

> That I should have been born in 1915, that I should be the contemporary of Auschwitz, Hiroshima and the Watts riots are things about which I was not first consulted. Yet they are events in which, whether I like it or not, I am deeply and personally involved. The "world" is not just a physical space traversed by jet planes and full of people running in all directions. It is a complex of responsibilities and options, made out of the loves, the hates, the fears, the joys, the hopes, the greed, the cruelty, the kindness, the faith, the trust, the suspicion of all. (*Conjectures of a Guilty Bystander*, the Abbey of Gethsemani, 1966, p. 161)

Sin and Grace (#1887-2029)

The roadblock on the way to happiness is that misuse of our freedom which we call sin. Generally we speak of sin as venial or mortal. We need to realize that these two differ not just in degree (one small, the other big), but in kind. In each case we *do* something qualitatively different. Venial sin is faltering in—but not altering—our fundamental commitment to God. Mortal sin, on the other hand, rejects that commitment.

Mortal sin always involves an action that is objectively serious and is chosen with full knowledge and freedom. We might say that it is the opposite of that turning toward God we call conversion: It is a turning away from God and our commitment to God's will.

Mortal sin is a fully human action, not something that takes us by surprise. It is generally preceded by a gradual breakdown of the inner unity of our persons. We lose that sense of interiority that makes us truly present to ourselves. The *Catechism* makes clear the importance of this interiority of spirit: Each of us must be sufficiently present to ourselves to hear and follow the voice of conscience. This demand for *inwardness* (interiority) is the more pressing, given that life often deprives us of opportunities for reflection, examination and self-awareness (#1779).

To end this brief discussion of aspects of Christian morality on the note of sin would give a false perspective. For what must be most prominent in our understanding of the Christian life is not sin but justification. Justification is that turning toward God that comes with the impulse of God's grace freely given to us by God's Holy Spirit. "Justification," the *Catechism* says, "is the *most excellent work of God's love*," which Saint Augustine held a greater act than the creation of the world (#1994). It is the work of God's Spirit enabling us to build a true interiority and inner unity. The Holy Spirit is the master of the interior life. By giving birth to our inmost self, justification involves the sanctification of the whole person (#1995).

Our joy as Christian people is knowing and in some measure experiencing that the power of grace is far greater than the power of sin. Saint Paul put it as well as anyone: "[W]here sin increased, grace abounded all the more" (Romans 5:20b).

Growing in Knowledge

1) Which is the greatest virtue? Why?

2) How do venial and mortal sins differ?

3) Is conscience a private matter? Why or why not?

4) What does it mean to be justified?

Growing in Faith

1) In what ways do you reflect the image of God?

2) What happy experiences have been a glimpse of what God

wants for you forever?

3) When in your life has love shown itself to be the strongest virtue?

4) Name an experience of grace in your life.

CHAPTER TEN

The Commandments and Christian Morality

The Ten Commandments state what is required in the love of God and love of neighbor.—Catechism of the Catholic Church, #2067

Recently, I saw an MTV promotion piece, a part of their "Free Your Mind Campaign." On the main street of a typical Old West town two cowboys, each armed with guns at both hips, walk toward one another. As the music mounts to a crescendo, they suddenly reach—not for their guns, but for one another. They embrace with a huge hug. The caption below the picture asks: "What did you expect them to do? Shoot one another?"

At a time when violence has become a commonplace experience and gun control appears to be impossible, that is exactly what we expected: that they would shoot one another. Our society has so conditioned us that, if we see a situation that seems to threaten violence, our minds are scarcely free to believe that it will not happen.

The gospel of Jesus Christ calls us to raise our expectations. It calls us to free our minds and purify our hearts so that we can think thoughts of peace, justice and love and act in such a way as to make them realities. For Jesus the Decalogue (the "ten words," or Ten Commandments) was a sacred part of the heritage of his people that held out a way for people to achieve freedom of mind and purity of heart.

The Ten Commandments (#2052-2082)

Given in Exodus 20:1-17 and in Deuteronomy 5:6-22, the Decalogue can only be understood in the terms of the particular context that brought the "ten words" into being. In the Hebrew Scriptures that context is the Exodus event, in which God liberated a people from Egyptian slavery. After this great deliverance, God enters into covenant with these people as a sign of the divine love and concern for them.

The Commandments, therefore, are not a series of do's and don'ts. They are covenant stipulations telling a liberated people how they can express their praise and thanks to the God who liberated them. The all-important prologue to the Commandments clearly places them in that context: "I am the LORD your God, who brought you out of the land of Egypt, out of the house of slavery" (Exodus 20:2). The deliverance was God's part in the covenant. It is followed by the covenant stipulations, which spell out for Israel the ways in which they are to respond to this wondrous, unmerited salvation. They are not the stern commands of a Lawgiver who demands obedience. They are the call of a Lover asking for a return of love.

That is why Jesus treats the Commandments with great respect. He is careful to say that he has not come to abolish the law. At the same time he seems to avoid saying that he came simply to obey it. The word he uses to express his attitude toward the law is "*fulfill*" (see Matthew 5:17). As the Sermon on the Mount makes clear, Jesus, without wavering in his reverence for the law, nonetheless reinterprets it. He does so to show, as the *Catechism* puts it, "the power of the Spirit at work in their letter" (see #2054). Jesus looks beyond external prescriptions to the inner spirit that motivates proper obedience to the law. He moved people to look beyond what the law *says* to what it *means*. Jesus transcends the law's letter to discover its deepest intent. The most striking examples of this are the great antitheses in the Sermon on the Mount: "You have heard...but I say to you...." For example: "You have heard that it was said to those of ancient times, 'You shall not murder....'But I say to you that if you are angry with a brother or sister, you will be liable to judgment' " (Matthew 5:21a, 22a).

When asked by a scribe what was the greatest of the commandments, Jesus replied: " 'You shall love the Lord your God with all your heart, and with all your soul, and with all your mind.' This is the greatest and first commandment. And a second is like it: 'You shall love your neighbor as yourself.' On these two commandments hang all the law and the prophets" (Matthew 22:37b-40). What Jesus did was to bring together a command from Deuteronomy 6:5 about love of God and a command from Leviticus 19:18 about love of neighbor to show that the Hebrew Scriptures themselves require, in the words of the *Catechism*, that "the Decalogue must be interpreted in light of this twofold yet single commandment of love, the fulfillment of the Law" (#2055). As Saint Paul put it: "love is the fulfilling of the law" (Romans 13:10b).

The Ten Commandments, considered simply as a reasonable expression of the way human beings should behave, may be viewed as a "privileged expression of the natural law" (#2070). Since they are discoverable by reason there is no strict need for revelation in order to know them. Since, however, we cannot always presume that beings who *can* reason will use that power, it is a boon to us to receive the Decalogue as part of God's revelation.

The First Tablet: Love of God

The Commandments are often depicted as two stone tablets engraved with Roman numerals. On one tablet are the first three Commandments, which spell out our relationship with God. The second holds the other seven, which govern our relationships with our neighbors.

The First Commandment (#2083-2141)

The First Commandment teaches the oneness of God. God alone is God: "I am the LORD, your God, who brought you out of the land of Egypt.... [Y]ou shall have no other gods before me" (Exodus 20:23; Deuteronomy 5:6, 7). We should note the personal dialogue of the Commandments ("I-thou"). This prologue telling what God did for the people is to be understood as a preface not just to the First Commandment, but to all of them. All are part of the dialogue of the Creator with creatures.

This first of the Commandments requires that we worship, obey and serve God. It forbids us to make images of God and thus it makes clear God's holiness, God's absolute transcendence. Nothing created can ever represent God. This Commandment does not forbid the veneration of images, namely, the use of religious images as ways to venerate the God to whom they point. It rather forbids the veneration of images that stops at the image itself or that would identify the image with God. Thus mental images (ideas, imaginings and so on) can become idols if we think that they can ever fully express the reality of God. But there are other ways of breaking this Commandment. When we give ultimate value to anything created, we are worshiping an idol. Business, success, achievement can all too easily be given an ultimacy in human life that belongs only to God and thus become the idols of today.

The Second Commandment (#2142-2167)

"You shall not make wrongful use of the name of the LORD your God" (Exodus 20:7a; Deuteronomy 5:11a) is about God's name and the veneration due to it. Just about the most spectacular event in the Hebrew Scriptures, rivaled only by the Exodus event itself, is the burning bush episode in Exodus 3. There God, at Moses' request, reveals the divine name. We don't really know the pronunciation of the name or its exact meaning. But reputable scholars believe that it has something to do with God's presence. The name assures Moses that God will be with him in the great events about to transpire in Egypt.

If we accept this meaning, then the name may be seen as an expression of God's intimate relationship with us. As the *Catechism* says, the gift of a name belongs to a relationship of confidence and intimacy (see #2143).

To ancient peoples, being able to name something or someone gave one a certain power over that which is named.

For instance, Adam's naming of the animals in Genesis 2:19-20 is a sign of his dominion over them. Knowing the divine name gave the people a certain power over God. The Second Commandment warns them not to abuse that power. The holiness of God's name is not to be abused by blasphemy (speaking ill of God) or by using God's name to confirm an oath that supports falsehood. Nor are oaths to be used in minor matters, for such a use of the divine name trivializes this gift of love and intimacy.

The Third Commandment (#2168-2195)
"Remember the sabbath day, and keep it holy" (Exodus 20:8; see also Deuteronomy 5:12a) recalls for the Jews creation and God's blessing of the seventh day. It also is a memorial of that central event of Israel's history: their liberation from the slavery of Egypt. It was, in addition, a sign of the covenant, for it is a day reserved for praising the God of the covenant. The sabbath as a day of rest was an important contribution to human culture. It was a day of refraining from work in order to be refreshed. It can be seen, therefore, as "a day of protest against the servitude of work and the worship of money" (#2172).

Christian faith has picked up the meaning attached to the sabbath and transferred it to Sunday, the first day of the week—the *Dies Dominica*, the Day of the Lord, "the day the Lord has made." As the first day of the week, the day of the Resurrection, the Lord's Day recalls the first creation; as the eighth day of the week it signifies the new creation ushered in by his Resurrection (see #2174).

Sunday is a day sacred to the Eucharist. The Sunday Eucharist differs from weekday Mass because it is a tradition that goes back to apostolic times. It is a more solemn celebration because all the community is expected to be there. It is a Mass of obligation, though an obligation that should flow more from love than from law (see #2177). Thomas Merton wrote these remarkable words about Sunday:

> Sunday is a day of contemplation, because it is sacred to the mystery of the Resurrection. Sunday is the "Lord's Day," not in the sense that, on one day out of

> the week, one must stop and think of him, but because it breaks into the ceaseless "secular" round of time with a burst of light out of a sacred eternity.... Sunday reminds us of the peace that should filter through the whole week when our work is properly oriented. (*The Inner Experience*, unpublished)

The *Catechism* reminds us that our Sunday leisure should not allow us to forget those who cannot rest because of poverty and destitution. Like Jesus, we see Sunday as an opportunity to put ourselves at times at the service of those in need (#2186).

The Second Tablet: Love of Neighbor

The remaining seven Commandments relate us to our sisters and brothers in the human community. They concern the fulfillment of what Jesus called the second commandment that is like the first: "Love your neighbor as yourself." The Fourth Commandment has to do with the duties we have toward others in society, beginning with the society of the family and moving out to other communities, even as far as the community of nations. The last six Commandments concern the respect we must give to life (Fifth), marriage (Sixth and Ninth), earthly possessions (Seventh and Tenth) and human speech (Eighth).

The Fourth Commandment (#2196-2257)

"Honor your father and your mother, so that your days may be long in the land that the LORD your God is giving you" (Exodus 20:12; see also Deuteronomy 5:16) is fundamentally about relationships. Most explicitly, it deals with the obligations of children to honor their parents. But, like the circles caused by a stone thrown into a lake, it broadens out to include the many relationships that constitute our lives.

The family is the place where relationships begin. As the *Catechism* says so well: "Authority, stability, and a life of relationships within the family constitute the foundations for freedom, security, and fraternity within society" (#2207).

The home is the first and most basic place of education and

personal formation; parents are the first and most important teachers of their children. In the home children learn the importance of mutual cooperation and community responsibilities. The home is the place where the life of faith and prayer has its beginnings.

As children grow into adults, they enter a wider range of relationships. As citizens of a nation, they are pledged to work for the common good (#2239). One *Catechism* statement that attracted the attention of reporters looking for "something new" has to do with civic responsibilities: to pay taxes, to vote, to share in the legitimate defense of the country (#2240).

Reaching beyond personal civic responsibilities, the *Catechism* speaks of the obligation of more prosperous nations to open their shores to immigrants and (while this is not stated, it certainly is implied) to be actively committed to the common good of the international community (#2241).

The Fifth Commandment (#2258-2330)

"You shall not murder" (Exodus 20:13; Deuteronomy 5:17) is concerned with the sacredness of life from its earliest beginning in the womb to its final cessation in death. Willful murder of an innocent person seriously contradicts human dignity. Abortion is a violation of this Commandment, because a person's right to life must be respected from the first moment of existence. Prenatal diagnostic techniques are morally acceptable as long as they respect fetal life and are used for healing and safeguarding it. The same principles apply to medical interventions on the human embryo. To produce human embryos for the purpose of research would be immoral.

Just as the beginning of life is sacred, so is its conclusion. Hence active intervention to terminate the life of a handicapped, sick or dying person is never acceptable. On the other hand, no one is obliged to continue medical treatments that are dangerous, extraordinary or disproportionate to the expected results. There is a big difference between intervening in a life process in order to bring about death and not intervening in the process of dying. The time comes when the most life-giving thing that can be done for a patient who is obviously dying is to switch from trying to cure (when that is clearly no longer possible) to giving the best possible care. This is the basic principle of a hospice: to give loving and gentle care. Cecily Saunders, founder of St. Christopher's Hospice in London, which follows that principle, was once asked by a visitor to St. Christopher's: "Where is your intensive care unit?" Her answer was: "Why, all our units are intensive care."

The Fifth Commandment extends beyond the relationships of individuals. It includes the task of working for peace. While still defending the possibility of legitimate self-defense, the Church's official teaching has become more and more skeptical about the age-old principles of the just war and even more skeptical about arms production and trafficking (see #2302-2317).

The Sixth Commandment (#2331-2400)

"You shall not commit adultery" (Exodus 20:14; see also Deuteronomy 5:18) has to do with a unique relationship: that between a man and a woman who commit themselves to one another in marriage for the whole of their lives. This Commandment prescribes chastity, which may be described as the integration of body-soul unity in the relationship of men and women to one another. Chastity has different meanings for different states of life. As Saint Ambrose said: "There are three forms of the virtue of chastity: the first that of spouses, the second that of widows, and the third that of virgins. We do not praise any one of them to the exclusion of the others.... This is what makes for the richness of the discipline of the Church" (#2349).

In marriage children are the fruit and fulfillment of a couple's love. As we saw in Chapter Eight, the teaching of the magisterium is that "each and every marriage act must remain open to the transmission of life" (#2366). At times couples who ardently want children seem unable to have them. For their sake it is important that research be undertaken to reduce human sterility. Such research must always be at the service of the person and must respect the design of the Creator. *Heterologous* artificial insemination and fertilization (the use of sperm or ovum from a third party) is gravely illicit. Spouses have the right to become parents only through one another.

Homologous artificial insemination and fertilization (where the sperm and ovum of husband and wife are combined, but outside of intercourse), is less objectionable, yet still morally unacceptable because the procreative act is separated from intercourse. In other words, the existence of the child is entrusted to science; it is not the result of the gift of husband and wife to each other.

The Seventh Commandment (#2401-2463)

"You shall not steal" (Exodus 20:15; see also Deuteronomy 5:19) commands, as the *Catechism* says, justice and charity in the stewardship of earthly goods and the fruits of human labor (see #2401). This Commandment is intended to protect the right to private property (acquired by work, inheritance or gift) and, at the same time, maintain the truth that the goods of creation are destined for the whole human race. It has also ecological implications: The goods of this earth are given to us to use, not to abuse. The social teachings of the Church, especially as expressed in papal encyclicals from Pope Leo XIII to Pope John Paul II, defend the rights of workers and call for an economic life that aims not only at multiplying goods and increasing profit or power, but primarily at serving individuals, the whole person and the entire human community (#2426). The wealth of the Church's teaching on social justice is too vast to be dealt with in detail here.

The Eighth Commandment (#2464-2513)

"You shall not bear false witness against your neighbor" (Exodus 20:16; see also Deuteronomy 5:20) forbids misrepresentation of the truth in all its forms, whether by individuals (through lying, perjury, calumny, and so on) or by government or mass media (through false management of information and advertising). It calls us to live the truth and to witness to it in the way we live.

Without truthfulness people cannot live together in community. For community presupposes that people can trust one another. Truthfulness keeps a just balance between what ought to be expressed and what ought to be kept secret, and involves both honesty and discretion (see #2469).

People have a right to proper information based on the truth. At a time when the communications media play so crucial a role in circulating information and forming people's thinking, there is a grave obligation on the part of the media to present the truth without bias and to respect the dignity and rights of individuals both in the search for news and in its dissemination. At the same time those who read or see or listen to the mass media must not allow themselves to become passive receivers of propaganda or slanted information. It is their duty to form enlightened and right consciences on the social, moral and political issues of the day.

The Ninth and Tenth Commandments (#2514-2557)
These two Commandments ("You shall not covet your neighbor's wife" and "You shall not covet your neighbor's house...or anything that belongs to your neighbor"; see Exodus 20:17; Deuteronomy 5:21) are concerned with the heart, out of which come both good and evil intentions. The Ninth calls for purity of heart to overcome lust; the Tenth for poverty of spirit to overcome greed. These two Commandments undergird the others, for keeping or breaking the others depends on what is in the human heart. As the *Catechism* expresses it, the Tenth Commandment concerns the intentions of the heart; with the Ninth, it covers all the Commandments (see #2534).

Indeed, in the long run, the Ten Commandments and the fulfillment to which Jesus brought them in his message that God loves us, and his command that we love as he has loved us brings us back to the "covenant of the heart" of which both Jeremiah and Ezekiel spoke.

> The days are surely coming, says the LORD, when I will make a new covenant.... I will put my law within them, and I will write it on their hearts; and I will be their God, and they shall be my people. (Jeremiah 31:31a, 33b)

Growing in Knowledge

1) What is the driving principle behind the Decalogue?

2) Why do we still honor the sabbath?

3) Are the Commandments personal or social? Why?

Growing in Faith

1) Compare God's giving the Commandments to the ways parents raise children.

2) Give an example of a law or rule losing its inner meaning.

3) What idols are held up for worship in our culture?

4) Overall, do you see the Commandments as positive or negative? Why?

CHAPTER ELEVEN

Christian Prayer

The Holy Spirit, whose anointing permeates our whole being, is the interior master of Christian prayer.
—Catechism of the Catholic Church, #2672

Six-year-old Mary Jane was saying her prayers before going to bed. At the end she mentioned with great earnestness a petition she was especially eager to have answered. Upon finishing her prayer, she added, as a kind of postscript, "By the way, I have mentioned this before."

Prayer is a universal phenomenon. Yet it can be a puzzling experience for those who are not clear about what it really is. The questions people have about prayer are many—the most crass, perhaps, implied in the cute little postscript Mary Jane added to her prayer: "Does it work?"

Such a question about prayer plunges us into the mystery of intercessory prayer: What does it mean to place our petitions before God? Are we asking God to change the divine plans for us, to change our life circumstances or to change our persons for the better? If we consider the last possibility (namely, that prayer asks God to change us) we arrive at a deeper level of the quest for the meaning of prayer.

A Journey of Faith

One thing is certain: Prayer is not just a passing phenomenon in human history. As far back as we are able to go, religion has always played an important role. And wherever religion is found, prayer is found. Prayer is religion's special language. At a level deeper than intercessory prayer, human beings experience the need to relate to the One who brought them into existence. One way they have discovered of seeking that relationship is prayer (#2566-2567).

Thus, life is a journey from God, who is our beginning. We journey also toward God, who is our destiny. Yet it would be a mistake to think that God shows up only at the beginning and the end, with perhaps an occasional appearance in between. No, we travel toward God *with* God: we are always in a relationship of intimacy with God. But more than that, we travel *in* God. We are in communion with God, which is to say that, though distinct from God, we are never separated from God. For separation from God would not just mean that we would cease to journey; we would cease to exist.

To say that we travel toward God with God and in God is to make clear that prayer is not first a human initiative, but a divine one. On life's journey it is God who first calls us. Tirelessly God invites us to that mysterious encounter which we have come to call prayer. In the words of the *Catechism*: "Whether we realize it or not, prayer is the encounter of God's thirst with ours" (#2560). What a fascinating experience it is when we do realize it!

Prayer is a many-faceted reality. The *Catechism* points to various aspects of prayer by leading us briefly through the Old Testament, the New Testament and the life story of the Church.

Prayer in the Old Testament (#2568-2597)

At the beginning of biblical history is the story of Abraham, which may be read as the story of growth in prayer. Abraham is called by God to leave his home and the certainties of life that home guarantees and to journey to a place that God will show him. His response is a prayer of action: obedient readiness and response to God's call. We are not told a single word that Abraham spoke in response to his call. His prayer was wordless, silent; it was, in the words of the *Catechism*, "attentiveness of the heart" (#2570).

As time goes on, one sees Abraham becoming more

comfortable with God. He welcomes God as a guest at Mamre. Then he is emboldened to speak out in intercession for the doomed cities of Sodom and Gomorrah, though his clever plan does not succeed.

Still later God makes enormous demands on him. He is asked to undergo a final purification of his relationship with God. He is told to sacrifice his only son, on whom he had pinned all his hopes for future descendants. His prayer becomes once again a silent acceptance of God's will. Indeed, it is a prayer that casts him in the likeness of God, who did not spare the only Son. What was true of Abraham can be true of us: Prayer can restore us to the likeness of God.

Moses is another figure of prayer set before us in the Old Testament. Once again we see God taking the initiative and calling Moses to save his people from Egyptian slavery. In the wondrous event of the burning bush (Exodus 3), God responds to Moses' prayer and reveals the divine self to Moses. This is the beginning of an intimacy with God unparalleled anywhere else in the Old Testament. Exodus puts it this way: God "used to speak to Moses face to face, as one speaks to a friend" (Exodus 33:11). Moses' intimacy with God unveils for us the meaning of contemplative prayer.

Moses is also a striking example of intercessory prayer, as he struggles with God to spare an often recalcitrant people.

Besides the many instances of the prayer of individuals, the Old Testament chronicles the important role prayer played in the lives of the people of Israel. Indeed, from them we receive that masterpiece of prayer that we call the Psalter or the Book of Psalms. The psalms present two kinds of prayer, personal and communal. Besides telling the history of God's people, the psalms reflect the varied human experiences of those who composed them. In the psalms we listen to God speaking to us, and we in turn speak to God. There is a simplicity and a spontaneity about these strong songs of Israel. They run the full gamut of human emotions: praise, thanks, fear, exultation, depression, anger, sorrow, joy.

Christians use the Psalter in the official prayer of the Church. When we pray the psalms we do so not just as individuals but as members of Christ. At times a particular psalm expresses exactly what we feel here and now. At other times its content may be foreign to the mood of the moment. Our mood may be joyful and the psalm may be sad. Yet if we pray the psalm as members of Christ, we can identify ourselves with all those who may be enduring great suffering at the time. Praying the psalms can give us, therefore, a deep sense of unity with our sisters and brothers.

Prayer in the New Testament (#2598-2622)

The New Testament, especially the Gospels (and among the Gospels, especially Luke), tells us how Jesus prayed and how he taught us to pray. Jesus, despite the constant pressure of the crowds, is often portrayed as going off to a quiet place to pray. Often he spent the whole night in prayer. What that prayer was like we cannot even imagine. It is an awesome picture: Jesus communing wordlessly with God, whose coming Kingdom he was proclaiming in his preaching.

Luke's Gospel tells us that Jesus is found in deep, prolonged prayer particularly before decisive moments in his life and mission: his baptism, the call of the Twelve, the Transfiguration, the Passion. Luke presents a moving word picture of Jesus at prayer before instructing the disciples about prayer: "He was praying in a certain place, and after he had finished, one of his disciples said to him: 'Lord, teach us to pray....' " (Luke 11:1). Notice that the disciples are careful not to interrupt Jesus' prayer. They are deeply moved as they see him so absorbed in God. Respectfully, they wait till his prayer is finished. Only then do they ask: "Lord, teach us to pray." They wanted to experience themselves this communion with God that was so obvious in Jesus' prayer.

Yet not all of Jesus' prayer was joyful resting in God. There are also the prayers of his Passion. The Letter to the Hebrews does not hesitate to tell us that "[i]n the days of his flesh, Jesus offered up prayers and supplications, with loud cries and tears, to the one who was able to save him from death..." (5:7a). The Gospels present his moving prayer in the garden of Gethsemane. It was an agonizing prayer begging release from the suffering he foresaw, yet submitting perfectly to God's will. But let no one fail to notice that it was a prayer in which he had to struggle.

Jesus took very seriously the disciples' request to be taught about prayer. In a sense his whole ministry was an effort to help people relate properly to God, which is to say an effort to teach them how to pray. Central to his teaching about prayer was an insistence on conversion of heart. As the *Catechism* says, "If our heart is far from God, the words of prayer are in vain" (#2562). Reconciliation with our sisters and brothers, love of enemies, prayer for persecutors and forgiveness of others are all preliminary conditions without which there is no authentic prayer.

Faith in God's goodness and watchfulness for God's entrance into our lives, a filial boldness (not unlike the somewhat petulant yet charming postscript of Mary Jane's prayer, mentioned earlier) are essential ingredients of prayer. This is what Jesus taught, as all through his ministry he responded not just to the request of a small group of disciples, but to the cry of a hurting world: "Lord, teach us to pray."

The New Testament also tells us of the prayer of Mary, the Mother of Jesus: her unconditional surrender of faith to the role God calls her to in the drama of salvation. There is also her bold call in the *Magnificat* for a new world in which false values will be overturned and the mighty overthrown. God's poor will inherit the Kingdom and peace and justice will reign upon the earth.

Prayer in the Life of the Church (#2623-2696)

A great wealth of prayers and teachings on prayer emerges from the experience of the Church through the ages. The contemplative prayer of the Desert Fathers, the writings of the Church Fathers, the Cistercian flowering of writings on prayer in the twelfth century, the mystical flourishing of the fourteenth century, the mystics of the post-Reformation period—all have made their contribution to a deeper understanding and appreciation of prayer in the life of the Christian community.

Running through all the diverse forms of Christian prayer are four fundamental stances we take toward God. First, there is *praise*, which sings God's glory—not for what God has done, but for who God is. We praise God for being God! *Thanksgiving* celebrates the wonders God has wrought for us so marvelously in creation and even more marvelously in God's works of salvation. *Petition* is prayer that acknowledges our creaturehood and our total dependence on God, to whom we owe all, who alone is good. *Intercession*, prayer on behalf of others, expresses our consciousness of communion with all God's people. It makes us realize that we are a communion of saints whose faith stories interrelate and intertwine with one another as we journey together toward God.

In the living tradition of prayer that we have inherited from the ages, prayer is addressed to the Father, to the Son and to the Holy Spirit. The most common formula of prayer (especially liturgical prayer) is "to the Father through the Son in the Holy Spirit." Jesus, God's Son and our brother, is the intermediary between God and us. He is the Intercessor. The Holy Spirit, whose anointing we receive when we are initiated into the Church, is the interior teacher of Christian prayer. The Holy Spirit is sent by the Father and the Son to lead us in the ways of prayer. Dear to the Christian tradition of prayer is this prayer to the Holy Spirit:

> Come, Holy Spirit,
> fill the hearts of your faithful
> and enkindle in them the fire of your love.

The Life of Prayer (#2697-2757)

It would be a mistake to see prayer simply as an action we engage in on occasion. It is not a fragment of our lives or a department of it. It is our life lived with a heart renewed. We must pray always—not in the sense of always saying prayers, but rather of always letting our lives be animated by our prayer. To live a life of prayer is to be conscious that at all times we are in the presence of God. This consciousness does not have to be explicit at all times; that is, we do not have to be paying attention to God's presence at all times. But regular fidelity to times of explicit prayer makes that divine presence a kind of aura or atmosphere in which we live, work and engage in ministry.

Kinds of Prayer

Times of explicit prayer find expression in various ways. Christian tradition has singled out three major ways of prayer: vocal prayer, meditative prayer and mental prayer.

Vocal Prayer. This prayer takes flesh in words. It is a necessary element of the life of prayer because we are body-spirit creatures who experience the need of expressing exteriorly what we feel within. It is necessary also because we need to use our whole being to praise God. The highest form of vocal prayer is liturgical prayer. All vocal prayer externalizes what is inside us. A vain repetition of words, with the heart unengaged, is not genuine prayer at all.

Meditative Prayer (Meditation). Meditation is above all a quest to discover what God wants of us and what response we need to make to the divine will. It involves discursive reasoning. The attentiveness required for such prayer is demanding. It helps to use a book, such as the Bible, liturgical texts or the works of spiritual writers. The holy icons, prominent in Eastern Christianity, are "books in color and prayer on wood" that, as we gaze upon them, can help deepen our faith and our commitment to Christian living.

We seek to make our own whatever it may be that we are meditating upon, striving in the process to deepen our faith convictions and our readiness to do God's will. In doing so we engage our mind, our imagination, our feelings. Yet meditation is not just an exercise in reflection. It is important that we bring our reflections to bear on our own life situation as we seek to answer the question: "Lord, what do you want me to do?" Our prayer should lead us to a deeper knowledge of God's love and our communion with God in Christ.

How do we *do* meditation? There are many and varied methods. We should choose whatever method helps us to be more attentive to God's presence and action in our lives. The important thing is that the way we pray lead us to a greater docility to the Spirit of God, who calls us to the imitation of

Christ. Some may find helpful the very ancient form of prayer known as *lectio divina*, which begins with reflection on the Scriptures and can lead to higher forms of prayer. Others may find the rosary a form of meditation suited to their needs. Still others will profit from the *Spiritual Exercises* of Saint Ignatius Loyola. We need to choose the form of prayer that fits our temperament and the growth we have achieved in our spirituality.

Mental Prayer or Prayer of the Heart. This form of prayer is called "mental" to distinguish it from prayer that makes use of words. It is, therefore, wordless prayer. The term "mental" is somewhat problematic. It seems to suggest a primary emphasis on the mind. But that is not what is intended. This form of prayer is "the simplest expression of the mystery of prayer" (#2713). The name "prayer of the heart" more properly fits it. For it is a prayer in which we let go of thoughts, imaginings and reflections in order to experience with deeper consciousness the presence of God. The "place" of this experience is our "center" or our heart. For it is by love, as well as by thought, that we come to know God.

This type of prayer also goes by the name of "contemplation." Contemplation is a "gazing" upon Christ: a gazing of faith. It is a simple resting in him or resting in God's presence.

It is also sometimes called "the prayer of quiet," "the prayer of silence," the "prayer of awareness," "centering prayer." The term *contemplation*, which for a long time seemed to express an elitist experience open only to a privileged few, has come to be seen as an experience that can be the normal flowering of our Baptism. The Trappist monk, Thomas Merton (1915-1968), did much through his writings to make contemplation a household word.

Difficulties in Prayer

The Christian life is a struggle to live the imperatives of the gospel. Our prayer life mirrors that struggle. "We pray as we live, because we live as we pray" (#2725). The "spiritual combat" of the Christian life is inseparable from the struggle of prayer.

Perhaps the most common problem of prayer is distraction. We come to prayer from a life that is busy, noisy and overengaged. We try to turn our heart to God, but our minds are so besieged by multitudes of thoughts, concerns, plans and projects that we almost forget that we are praying. To deal with distractions in prayer, we need to deal with the lives we live. If we tend to live fragmented, overly busy, frantic lives, distractions will inevitably intrude. We do indeed pray as we live.

Still, we must not become unduly anxious about our distractions. To some degree, given the life situations in which most of us have to function, distractions are inevitable. What is important, above all, is daily fidelity to prayer as well as the realization that, in ultimate terms, it is the grace of God that makes prayer a possibility. We do our best to respond to that grace and then place ourselves confidently in God's hands. We need often to recall Paul's words: "Likewise the Spirit helps us in our weakness; for we do not know how to pray as we ought, but that very Spirit intercedes with sighs too deep for words. And God, who searches the heart, knows what is the mind of the Spirit, because the Spirit intercedes for the saints according to the will of God" (Romans 8:26-27).

As we grow in the life of prayer, many of the things that once disturbed us about prayer no longer do so. Why doesn't God seem to answer my prayers? Does prayer really work? Does it make any difference in my life? Such questions no longer have the importance they once had. It is not that the questions go away or that we have answers that satisfy. It is rather that we no longer need answers to questions that are so speculative. They occupy, after all, but a small place in a life that is enveloped by the boundless Love that we meet in prayer. And that surely is satisfaction enough.

Growing in Knowledge

1) What is the value of intercessory prayer?

2) How did prayer affect Jesus' life?

3) What are the three essential ingredients of prayer?

4) What are the four fundamental stances toward God?

GROWING IN FAITH

1) Compare your life journey with Abraham's.

2) What are the obstacles to prayer in your life?

3) With what type of prayer are you most comfortable?

4) What does Jesus' experience of prayer tell you about your own?

CHAPTER TWELVE

The Lord's Prayer

The Lord's Prayer is truly the summary of the whole gospel.—Tertullian

Several years ago I directed a retreat at Saint Catherine's, an Anglican retreat house on the east side of London. I was told that both Anglicans and Roman Catholics would be making the retreat. After the first presentation, I invited the retreatants to spend some time in silent prayer, at the end of which we said the Lord's Prayer together. After the prayer was over, I said, "I see there are more Anglicans here than Roman Catholics." A show of hands indicated that I was correct: About two-thirds of the retreatants were Anglican. Someone asked me how I knew. I answered that it was the slower pace with which they said the Lord's Prayer. Roman Catholics tend to speed-pray this beautiful prayer; Anglicans set a more deliberate pace. On this occasion, because of their number, they were able to slow down their more haste-prone co-retreatants.

Most of us Catholics say the Lord's Prayer quite often—perhaps several times a day. More times than I want to admit, I say the Lord's Prayer and then afterwards I am not even sure that I said it. We all have to learn that, just as you can't make friends in a hurry or grow plants in a hurry, so we cannot rush through prayer and expect to meet God in it. I am not suggesting that we must always have a lot of time in which to pray. I am saying that whatever time we may have, we should pray slowly, deliberately and reflectively. Better to say half the Lord's Prayer attentively than to rattle through the whole of it without attention (#2766).

The Prayer of the Church (#2765-2772)

The Lord's Prayer is a beautiful gift that Jesus has given us. It is the first gift the Church gives to the catechumens as they prepare for the sacraments of initiation. Born anew in the living waters of Baptism, catechumens learn to invoke their Father by the Word God always hears. Most of the commentaries on the Lord's Prayer written by the Church Fathers—and there are many—are addressed to the catechumens or to the newly baptized. The Lord's Prayer is the prayer of the Church *par excellence*. An integral part of the Divine Office, it also has a place of prominence in the Eucharist, coming between the Eucharistic Prayer and the Communion.

Some people have thought that there are Protestant and Catholic versions of the Lord's Prayer, with the Protestant version adding the words: "For the kingdom, the power and the glory are yours now and forever." This doxology (a brief expression of praise) is not found in the New Testament, but it appeared very early in liturgical usage—long before the Protestant Reformation (#2760). Many Christian Churches use it. The present Roman Missal adds it to the Lord's Prayer after developing the last petition of the prayer ("Deliver us from evil") in such a way as to place that cry for deliverance in the perspective of waiting "in joyful hope for the coming of our Savior Jesus Christ" (#2855).

'Our Father' (#2777-2793)

Though we often say the Lord's Prayer privately, it is first and foremost the prayer of the Christian community. The *Catechism* quotes Saint John Chrysostom as saying that the Lord teaches us to pray for our brothers and sisters in community by inviting us to say not "*my* Father who art in heaven," but "*our* Father" (#2768). Praying "Our Father" helps protect us against a narrow individualism. It reminds us that this prayer is the heritage of all the baptized. In spite of the divisions that may exist among Christians, there is one God and Father of us all whom we all invoke in the Lord's Prayer. It should remind all Christians of their summons to strive for Christian unity. Indeed, praying "Our Father" reminds us that

God is Father of all peoples and of the whole of creation. Hence our prayer includes all who do not know God: we pray that all may be gathered into one.

'Who Art in Heaven' (#2794-2796)
"In heaven" refers not to a place, but to a way of being. It is meant to suggest not remoteness on God's part, but rather the divine majesty: God's being in perfect glory. This God of majesty is at the same time close to the lowly and humble of heart. The *Catechism* quotes Saint Augustine: " 'Our Father who art in heaven' is rightly understood to mean that God is in the hearts of the just, as in his holy temple. At the same time, it means that those who pray should desire the one they invoke to dwell in them" (#2794).

The Seven Petitions (#2803-2806)

Addressing God as our Father who is close to us gives us the courage to address our petitions to God. There are seven in all. In the first three petitions we turn toward God, whom we love. We express our burning desire for the glory of God's name, for the coming of God's Kingdom, for the carrying out of God's will. In none of these petitions do we mention ourselves. It is in this very self-forgetfulness that "we are strengthened in faith, filled with hope and set aflame by charity" (#2806).

The four remaining petitions concern our basic needs: (1) to be fed ("give us daily bread"); (2) to be healed ("forgive us as we forgive"); (3) to deal with temptation; (4) to overcome evil and achieve our final victory of eternal life with God.

'Hallowed Be Thy Name' (#2807-2815)
To "hallow" literally means to "make holy." Clearly this is not the sense that is meant here. We do not make God's name holy, but we pray that the holiness of God's name may be recognized, that it may be treated and respected as holy, that it may be honored. The holiness of God is the inaccessible center of God's eternal mystery, partly revealed in creation, partly revealed in history, fully revealed in the mystery of Jesus (see

#2809-2812). Jesus told his disciples that "no one knows the Son except the Father, and no one knows the Father except the Son and anyone to whom the Son chooses to reveal him" (Matthew 11:27b). Because of the limits of our ability to comprehend, however, even Jesus cannot fully reveal God to us. God always remains a mystery that we can never name. When we honor God's ineffable name, we honor God.

This petition is thoroughly rooted in the Old Testament, where ancient Israelite covenants were solemnly sealed by invoking the name of God. The prophets often spoke of Israel's sins as dishonoring God's name. Restoring exiled Israel to its land is God's honoring the divine name: "O house of Israel...I am about to act...for the sake of my holy name, which you have profaned among the nations.... [A]nd the nations shall know that I am the LORD...when through you I display my holiness before their eyes. I will take you from the nations, and gather you from all the countries, and bring you into your own land" (Ezekiel 36:22-24).

'Thy Kingdom Come' (#2816-2821)

The Greek word *basileia* has three different but closely related meanings: "royalty" (an abstract noun), "kingdom" (a concrete noun) and "reign" (an action noun).

The Kingdom of God is ahead of us. It is brought near to us in the Incarnate Word of God and proclaimed in the preaching of the gospel. Though a reality of the future, it becomes radically present in the world in the death and resurrection of Jesus. In the Paschal Mystery, the reign of sin and death is broken and the reign of God fully established in Jesus. In him the Kingdom *has* come.

When all God's people are fully incorporated into the Paschal Mystery of Jesus, the reign of God will prevail over all. Then Christ will return in glory and hand the Kingdom over to God, and God will be all in all (see 1 Corinthians 15:24-28). This is the Kingdom come in glory. This is the end-time, when the plan of God will be fully realized.

The Second Vatican Council made clear that we must distinguish earthly progress from the growth of the Kingdom. But distinction does not mean separation. Human triumphs and the works produced by human talents and energy are, the Council says, "a sign of God's greatness and the flowering of his mysterious design" (*Constitution on the Church in the Modern World*, #34). Hence earthly progress "is of vital concern to the kingdom of God, insofar as it can contribute to the better ordering of human society" (*Constitution on the Church in the Modern World*, #39).

'Thy Will be Done on Earth as It Is in Heaven' (#2822-2827)
This third petition is a kind of appendage to the first two. For it indicates the way in which God's name will be hallowed and God's Kingdom will come. "Thy will be done" quite clearly reminds us of Jesus' prayer in the garden of Gethsemane. It reminds us also of Jesus' words: "Not everyone who says to me, 'Lord, Lord,' will enter the kingdom of heaven, but only the one who does the will of my Father in heaven" (Matthew 7:21). This petition joins us in a communion of intercession with Mary, the Mother of God, and with all who please God because they always desire to do God's will.

What is the will of God? In most general terms it is summed up in Jesus' command to "love one another as I have loved you" (John 15:12b). In ultimate terms the will of God is to bring to fulfillment the "mystery" God has chosen to make known to us in Christ. That mystery is the divine plan to break down the barriers between Jews and Gentiles. It was God's plan to restore all things to harmony and oneness in Christ. When this divine plan achieves completion, then God's name will indeed be hallowed and God's Kingdom will have come.

It is through obedience to the divine will that the divine plan is accomplished. Jesus, Son of God and son of Mary, is the model of perfect obedience. He always did the will of God. This does not mean it was easy or something automatic for him. No, he was human, and had to struggle to achieve perfect submission to God's will. The Letter to the Hebrews speaks of this struggle: "Although he was a Son, [Jesus] learned obedience through what he suffered..." (Hebrews 5:8). The New English Bible offers this translation: "He learned obedience *in the school of suffering*" (emphasis added).

That is the school in which we too have to learn obedience

to the demands of God's will. In order to obey God's will, we first have the task of discerning what the divine will is. Helpful guidelines are offered to us in the Commandments and in the teachings of the magisterium. But there are many situations in which, formed by these guidelines and listening to the Holy Spirit present within us, we have to use our own powers of discernment: in choosing a vocation in life, in deciding how to deal with a situation of estrangement from another person, in knowing how we appropriately express the love we owe to others in a particular case, and in many other situations which no rules can foresee.

"Heaven" is understood here not as the abode of the blessed, but as the "area" above the earth where sun, moon, stars and planets obey the will of God. The brilliant second-century Christian writer, Origen, gives these words a spiritual meaning. *Heaven*, he suggests, refers to Christ, who always does God's will; and *earth* refers to the Church, striving to do the will of God but not always succeeding. Hence we need to pray that the Church obey the will of God as Jesus does.

'Give Us This Day Our Daily Bread' (#2828-2837)

As God's trusting children, we simply ask that God care for us and our needs. In asking for "daily bread," we of course have in mind our need for physical nourishment. But "daily bread" includes also the spiritual goods and blessings we hope to receive from God.

To ask for our daily bread is to remind ourselves that half of the world goes to bed hungry for lack of bread. The petition involves, therefore, an acceptance of our responsibility to be in solidarity with our sisters and brothers who are victims of poverty and oppression. We commit ourselves to work to rectify the structures of society so that they may serve the needs of all, not just of a select group. The *Catechism* forcefully reminds us that "there are no just structures without people who want to be just" (#2832). We cannot, it tells us, isolate this petition of the Lord's Prayer from the parables of the poor man, Lazarus, and of the Last Judgment (Luke 16:19-31 and Matthew 25:31-46; see #2831).

This petition also evokes another picture of a hunger that

many people suffer: a hunger for the word of God. We are reminded of the words Jesus quoted in the desert of his temptations: "One does not live by bread alone,/ but by every word that comes from the mouth of God" (Matthew 4:4b; see Deuteronomy 8:3b). We are reminded too of those moving words of the prophet Amos about a famine on the earth: "not a famine of bread, or a thirst for water,/ but of hearing the words of the LORD" (Amos 8:11). As disciples of Jesus, we are called to proclaim the Good News of God's word to the poor.

Finally, this petition for our daily bread is a request for the Bread of Life that Jesus gives us in the Eucharist—the foretaste of the eternal banquet prepared for us when the Kingdom comes in its fullness.

'And Forgive Us Our Trespasses, as We Forgive Those Who Trespass Against Us' (#2838-2845)

Making this petition calls for courage. We ask God to forgive us only to the degree that we forgive others. We are saying in effect that if we don't forgive, we have no right to receive forgiveness. Jesus makes an even stronger point in the parable about the slave who is forgiven a huge amount of money owed by him to the master, but then refuses to forgive a small amount owed to him by a fellow-slave. When the master hears of the man's hard-heartedness, he has him cast into prison. Jesus' comment on the parable is: "So my heavenly Father will also do to every one of you, if you do not forgive your brother or sister from your heart" (Matthew 18:35).

The parable challenges us to put ourselves in the shoes of a fellow who has received what amounts to infinite mercy and who refuses to show the slightest mercy to a fellow-servant.

But we must not think that Jesus is telling us that our God is a God of retaliation who says to us: "If you don't forgive, I'll show you: I won't forgive you either." This would be to misunderstand the God Jesus revealed to us: a God who always forgives. The point Jesus is making is much more profound. God *cannot* forgive us unless we forgive. For unforgiving hearts are hardened hearts; because they refuse to impart forgiveness, they are incapable of receiving it.

Suppose a friend asked you to plant a flower for her in a

huge block of concrete. You might very much want to do this, because you love your friend. But you are unable to do so, for concrete is too hard a material to receive the roots of the flower. In a similar manner, forgiveness cannot be received into an unforgiving heart. Such a heart is a hardened heart. There are times when spiritually we need "open-heart surgery." We need to have our sometimes hardened hearts opened by God's grace, so that God's love and forgiveness may flow into us and through us to others. "Others," as Jesus makes clear to us in the Sermon on the Mount, includes enemies as well as friends. There can be no limits to our forgiveness, as there are no limits to God's.

'And Lead Us Not into Temptation' (#2846-2849)

The word translated "temptation" may also mean "trial" or "test." Clearly God does not *lead* us into temptation, trial or testing. The sense of the Greek verb, which cannot be conveyed in a single English equivalent, is best rendered, "Do not allow us to be led into temptation." We find a similar expression in Jesus' words in the garden of Gethsemane where, after praying the first time, he finds the disciples asleep and says: "Stay awake and pray that you may not come into the time of trial" (Matthew 26:41).

Yet even this translation does not carry the full meaning of this petition. We know that temptations, trials and tests are experiences in life that we have to face. We cannot dodge them all. So what are we really praying for? As far as temptations to sin and evil are concerned, we pray that we may have the strength not to succumb to them. As for trials and tests, we pray that through God's Spirit we may have the grace to discern between those which can be sources of spiritual growth to us if we face them resolutely and those that lead to sin and spiritual deterioration if we allow them to overcome us.

'But Deliver Us From Evil' (#2850-2854)

In the final petition of the Lord's Prayer we ask deliverance from all the evils that weigh us down: the distress, the alienation, the anxiety that life inevitably brings. We know that we have to struggle with evil in ourselves and in our world—evil that so often is beyond our comprehension. Yet at the same time we know, as we have heard proclaimed in the *Catechism*, that Jesus the Christ has won deliverance for us. Our hope for full participation in that deliverance is linked with his glorious coming to give the world back to God. This sense of a present experience of deliverance from evil joined to ultimate victory is beautifully expressed in the prayer of the Mass that follows the last petition of the Lord's Prayer: "Deliver us, Lord, from every evil, and grant us peace in our day. In your mercy keep us free from sin and protect us from all anxiety as we wait in joyful hope for the coming of our Savior, Jesus Christ."

'Amen' (#2856)

We conclude the prayer with a ringing confirmation of all that it says. *Amen* cries out: "Yes, I really mean it. Yes, I want to mean it ever more deeply."

Since the Amen concludes not only the Lord's Prayer, but likewise the *Catechism*, it can be also our yes to all that has been revealed by God and proclaimed by Jesus. We affirm our desire and determination to imitate the stance toward God and humanity which Paul so beautifully ascribes to our Lord: "...Jesus Christ, whom we proclaimed among you...was not...'Yes' and 'No'; but in him it is always 'Yes' " (2 Corinthians 1:19).

GROWING IN KNOWLEDGE

1) What are the three meanings of *Kingdom* in the Lord's Prayer?

2) To what does "daily bread" refer?

3) Why must we forgive in order to be forgiven?

4) Does God lead us into temptation?

GROWING IN FAITH

1) How do you usually think of God—as very close or as far off in heaven? Why?

2) Name a time when an experience of suffering helped you to grow in faith.

3) Can you recall a liberating experience of forgiveness?

4) What is your favorite part of the Lord's Prayer?